THE LEXINGTON SCHOOL FOR THE DEAF
EDUCATION SERIES

Teaching Arithmetic to Deaf Children
Veronica O'Neill

Teaching Reading to Deaf Children
Beatrice Ostern Hart

Science for Deaf Children
Allan Leitman

A Parents' Program in a School for the Deaf
Paul Rotter

Vocabulary Norms for Deaf Children
Toby Silverman-Dresner and George R. Guilfoyle

Listening: Notes From a Kindergarten Journal
Claire Blatchford

Teaching Speech to Deaf Children
Eleanor Vorce

Educational Strategies for the Youngest Hearing Impaired
Children (0 to 5 Years of Age)
Marya P. Mavilya and Bernadette R. Mignone

Developed at The Lexington School for the Deaf
30th Avenue and 75th Street
Jackson Heights, N.Y. 11370

Teaching Reading to Deaf Children

LEXINGTON SCHOOL
FOR THE DEAF

BEATRICE OSTERN HART

Copyright © 1962, 1978
By the Alexander Graham Bell Association for the Deaf, Inc.

Revised Edition

The Alexander Graham Bell Association for the Deaf, Inc.
3417 Volta Place, N.W.
Washington, D.C. 20007

Library of Congress Catalogue Card Number 78-50668
ISBN 0-88200-117-5

The Author:

Mrs. Beatrice Ostern Hart, a graduate of Brooklyn College, New York City, earned her M.A. degree in Special Education at Teachers College, Columbia University. After completing her training in the teaching of hearing-impaired children, she taught at all levels—from elementary through high school—at the Lexington School for the Deaf. As Language and Reading Supervisor she was instrumental in shaping the language arts program that characterizes and distinguishes the Lexington School.

Teachers throughout the country are familiar with Mrs. Hart's ideas and work in language and reading. Her workshops, her participation in professional conventions, and her articles in *The Volta Review* have influenced countless educators. As instructor in the Special Education Department of Teachers College, Columbia University, she has imbued many teachers-in-training with the philosophy and methodology of the natural method.

Mrs. Hart is the co-author of *Word Wise, A Creative Language Arts Workbook.*

Preface to the second edition

Beatrice Ostern Hart's revision of *Teaching Reading to Deaf Children* will provide for the current generation of deaf children and the upcoming teachers of the deaf what her original book has accomplished for the past 15 years. Those thousands of children and hundreds of teachers owe her a great deal, and the Lexington School's proudest claim is that it helped to develop this outstanding philosophy and program. I join with Dr. Clarence O'Connor, Superintendent Emeritus of the Lexington School, in sharing our personal pride and educational products with all of you.

Leo E. Connor, Ed.D.
Executive Director
January 1978

Foreword

The observation is frequently made by those undertaking investigations of various phases of the problems related to deafness that there is an appalling lack of published material in this area of exceptionality. Invariably, then, following this observation, comes the request for a bibliography on deafness or the location of centers where such publications dealing with various facets of hearing impairment may be secured. Our most reliable and prolific sources of help have always been the Alexander Graham Bell Association for the Deaf and the *American Annals of the Deaf.* Too frequently, however, the material available for distribution is in the form of reprints dealing in general terms with some particular and limited aspect of deafness.

The request most frequently received at the Lexington School, both from those who have visited the school and from those who have written to us, has been for outlines that will help administrators and supervising teachers set educational goals for their deaf children and which will help classroom teachers achieve these goals more effectively. These requests have usually been made in the form of a question—"Do you have a course of study covering the program offered at the Lexington School and, if so, may I have a copy?"

To meet this obvious professional need, various members of the Lexington School staff have been working for ten years on the development of a series of monographs to be published by the Alexander Graham Bell Association for the Deaf under the name of "The Lexington School for the Deaf Education Series." It is our hope that this series will provide more than that usually contained in a standard course of study. Each unit of the series will outline in detail not only the goals we set for our pupils here at the Lexington School in the particular phase of our program with which the monograph deals, but will also describe activities, techniques, and devices we have found particularly effective through the years in achieving these goals. Each publication will represent the best thinking of selected teachers skilled in particular subject areas, edited by the Curriculum Committee, and coordinated and brought into final form by a master teacher. Each will include, as well, reference to the best information available in the literature of the general education field.

If deaf children can be taught to master reading skills, reading can be not only a highly rewarding recreational activity for them but also an avenue for continued growth and enrichment. The road to reading success is not an easy one for the deaf student. It requires patience and fortitude. And it requires a teacher who is thoroughly knowledgeable in both curriculum and educational psychology.

This monograph presents teachers of the deaf with a developmental program for teaching reading. It contains a philosophy as well as a plan. The emphasis throughout is on the purpose rather than the process of reading, or as Betts has said, on reading to learn rather than learning to read. Suggestions are made for activities at each level, from the nursery through the advanced, through which children can enjoy reading and develop the skills they need.

Only when the teacher of the deaf has a sound knowledge of teaching techniques can he adapt these approaches to meet the special needs of deaf pupils. If the reading program in schools for the deaf is successful, deaf children will gain an invaluable tool for the enjoyment of life.

It is hoped that this monograph will contribute to this end.

Clarence D. O'Connor
Superintendent Emeritus
(1962)

Table of Contents

1. The reading process

Learning to read is a formidable task for most children, a frustrating task for many children, an impossible task for some children. No less literate a person than the noted author John Steinbeck poignantly describes his own early experience with reading as follows: "I remember that words—written or printed—were devils, and books, because they gave me pain, were my enemies." With historical perspective, he points up the universality of his personal experience: "Some people there are who, being grown, forget the horrible task of learning to read. It is perhaps the greatest single effort that the human undertakes, and he must do it as a child. An adult is rarely successful in the undertaking—the reduction of experience to a set of symbols. For a thousand thousand years these humans have existed and they have only learned this trick—this magic—in the final ten thousand of the thousand thousand."[1]

Steinbeck succeeds beautifully in making us understand why the problem of illiteracy continues to plague us on such a massive scale. If it is taking all of mankind so very long (many of the languages in use today still exist only in spoken form) to achieve the miracle of written language, why should we expect individual humans to make this leap without travail? The fact is that they don't. UNESCO reports that two-fifths of the world's adult population (15 and over)

[1] Adapted from the introduction to John Steinbeck's *The Acts of King Arthur and His Noble Knights.* New York: Farrar, Straus & Giroux, 1976.

1

cannot read or write. In parts of Asia and Africa illiteracy ranges around 85 percent to 95 percent, and even in such a highly developed nation as the United States there were in 1965 more than eight million adults over the age of 25 who could not read and write.

Special Problems of the Deaf

If learning to read is so difficult for the "normal" child, how much more difficult must it be for the child who is handicapped by deafness? Not only do achievement test scores testify to the pitifully poor progress deaf children make in mastering reading, but the daily evidence in schools and homes indicates that the vast majority of deaf children are uninterested in opening a book, or frustrated if they do. Although we have become increasingly concerned about the large numbers of school children who have trouble with reading, actually most hearing children do learn to read successfully. This is not so with deaf children; only a small minority achieve proficiency in reading, while the majority do not manage to attain more than a fourth grade reading level. To understand why failure in reading is "normal" for the deaf child we have to ask: What about reading makes it frustrating for the deaf child? or What about deafness makes it antipathetic to reading?

The linguists can help us answer these questions. "To begin with," says Ignatius G. Mattingly, "listening appears to be a more natural way of perceiving language than reading" (Kavanagh & Mattingly, 1972). Spoken language is a primary linguistic activity, whereas "reading is parasitic on language" (Liberman, in Kavanagh, 1968). "Spoken words are symbols for things, events and ideas, and written words are symbols for spoken words" (Gibson, in Kavanagh & Mattingly, 1972). In other words, you must know language before you can read. Hearing children learn to understand and use spoken language naturally and easily as part of a maturational process. They do not need to be taught. By the time they approach the task of learning to read at the age of 5 or 6, they are sophisticated language users and have mastered to an astonishing degree the semantic and syntactic structure of their language. But they do not read automatically; they must be taught. To learn to read they must apply their knowledge of language to the written words, which are the symbols for the spoken words they already know. "The process of learning to read in one's native langauge is the process of transfer from the auditory signs for language signals, which the child has already learned, to the new visual signs for the same signals. This process of transfer is not the learning of the language code or of a new language code; it is not the learning of a new or different set of language signals. It is not the learning of new 'words' or of new grammatical structures, or of new meanings. These are all matters of the language signals which he has on the whole already learned so well that he is not conscious of their use" (Fries, 1962).

As every teacher of the deaf is painfully aware, this does not describe the reading process of the deaf child. Learning to read is more difficult for deaf children because they are not just learning to read; they are also learning new language at the same time. Deaf children do not learn to understand and use language as a natural maturational process; they must be taught language deliberately. And whatever medium or techniques are used, progress for the profoundly deaf child is necessarily slow and painstaking. The eye, despite everything, is simply not as proficient a channel as the ear for language learning. Thus, when deaf children begin the process of learning to read at the age of 5 or 6, their linguistic skills are generally quite limited. Their vocabulary is, on the whole, small, highly concrete, and deficient in function words. And they are in the very beginning stages of experimenting with and generalizing the morphological and syntactic rules of language. This means that there is almost inevitably a gap between the deaf child's actual language level and the language level of the reading material that the child is attempting to interpret.

Just in order to get some feel for what reading a story might be like for the young deaf child, try reading the following simple selection from the Scott, Foresman Reading Systems, Level 4, Set A, in which I have substituted nonsense syllables for some of the words that the young deaf child is not likely to know. I have also distorted the questions in the same way to give some idea of why it is so hard to check on comprehension.

JOHN AND HIS DRUM

John had a drum, a flid big drum.
It made a flid big shole when he krin it.
John liked the drum.

From SCOTT FORESMAN READING SYSTEMS, Special Practice Books, Level 4, Set A by Ira E. Aaron, A. Sterl Artly, Kenneth S. Goodman, et. al. Copyright © 1971 by Scott, Foresman & Co. Reprinted by permission.

But John's father brunce like it.
His mother brunce like it.
His little sister brunce like it.
The shole made pel cry.

John wanted to find a voke to play his drum.
So one day he foon it to school.
But the teacher brunce like the drum at school.
He made John take it lunt home.

The trun day John foon his drum to the park.
But the birds brunce like it.
They holm pire.
The dogs brunce like it.
They eltip to rane.

John was sad.
He put his drum in his wagon.
He renule to walk home.
Then he saw a good voke to play his drum.

John krin his drum fip hard fip he doush.
He krin it prept, and he krin it prept.
Flin was chelp the doon voke for John and his drum.

1. Lanch tix John want to find?
2. Tump tix he look?
3. Tump was the hool voke to play his drum?

An even more important explanation of why deaf children have
trouble learning to read is that learning language by eye rather than
by ear not only means that vocabulary growth is slow and mastery of
grammar comes late, but that the sound system of their language
largely eludes deaf children. They get no clues from the phonological
or from the suprasegmental (pitch, stress, juncture) elements in the
language system. In fact, I am inclined to believe that deaf children
are slower to master the lexical and grammatical system precisely
because they cannot make use of these sound clues. We know that
hearing children respond to and use intonational patterns before they
understand and use words (Lewis, 1951). Written language offers

only limited graphic clues (punctuation marks, quotation marks, italics) to the intonational patterns of the language presented. The hearing child, having automatically absorbed the sound system, applies this knowledge to the printed word, grouping words into phrases, putting stress on the syllables and words where it belongs. It takes deaf children a long, long time (if ever) before they can do this. If you would like to get some sense of what depriving language of suprasegmental clues might do to comprehension, try this little experiment. Pick up any book and select any paragraph at random. Read it aloud, deliberately distorting suprasegmental elements of the sound system—do not phrase groups of words properly; avoid accenting the key words in a phrase or the key syllable in a word; read flatly without variations of pitch. Then reread the paragraph as you would normally. This may give a small indication of why the printed word is different for the deaf child than for the hearing child.

In trying to understand "why should reading be, by comparison with listening, so perilous a process," Mattingly says "reading depends ultimately on linguistic awareness and the degree of this awareness varies considerably from person to person . . . There must be a minimum level required, and perhaps not everyone possesses this minimum" (Kavanagh & Mattingly, 1972). It would certainly make sense that deaf children would have trouble with reading until they acquire the minimum level of linguistic awareness required, and that those children who never achieve this minimum level simply do not ever learn to read to any meaningful extent. This explains something that appears as a common phenomenon when standardized reading scores of deaf children are examined. Average scores at successive age levels reveal fractional increments and severe retardation, averaging about four years, at each age level. But when the averages are analyzed by age and grade it can be noted that many young deaf children are achieving higher scores than some much older deaf children, and that the low increments from age to age are heavily contributed to by those children who are the failed readers. These are the children who fail to achieve minimal language awareness and consequently never achieve more than third or fourth grade reading levels.

Approaches to Reading

Learning to read is a highly complex process involving a series of perceptual, linguistic, and conceptual skills. Traditionally there have been two major approaches to the teaching of reading. One approach, based on the linguists' concept that the printed word is a symbol for the spoken word, assumes that if children can be taught to perceive the relations between printed and spoken symbols they will automatically use their already existing knowledge of language to understand what they decipher. The specific methods within this approach vary, but they all teach techniques of word recognition by systematically presenting first the regularities, and then the irregularities, between spoken and written English. (Flesch stresses phonics skills; Bloomfield and Barnhardt introduce patterns of letters and sounds disregarding meaning; Pitman rewrites letters in ITA to standardize the sound-letter relationship. The structuralists stress not only the phonological system, but also the linguistic meanings contributed by stress, pitch, grammar, and syntax.)

The second approach regards written language as an alternate means of communication and stresses content more than form. Children are taught to take meaning from written language by relating the ideas to their own experience and knowledge.

But since reading is, as Steinbeck says, "the reduction of experience to a set of symbols," in reality teachers hardly ever use one approach exclusively. They mix elements of both, teaching phonics and word recognition skills when needed, and working on comprehension skills simultaneously. In this way, children learn both to decode the symbols and to interpret the experience conveyed in these symbols. The question for teachers of the deaf is: Should reading be taught to the deaf child the same way it is taught to the hearing child, i.e., is reading the same process for the deaf child as it is for the hearing child? The answer, unfortunately, has to be yes and no. The deaf child, like the hearing child, must learn to interpret written symbols in order to understand the experience conveyed by them. But, whereas the hearing child can relate the written symbols to known sound symbols, it is questionable whether the deaf child does this. Those deaf children who are taught exclusively by oral-aural techniques, using speech and residual hearing, and who are taught phonics skills later on when they begin to learn to read may parallel the process that hearing children follow. However, most deaf children, including many taught in the oral-aural tradition, undoubtedly do not use phonological coding at all. Most deaf children learn to interpret both spoken and written language visually. Research findings (e.g., by Furth and by Rosenstein) indicate that deaf children are excellent users of visual clues, so teaching them to decipher the printed word using visual rather than phonological or auditory techniques should present no problem (unless the deafness is accompanied by other handicaps that interfere with visual perception).

A Visual Process

In other words, it is possible (and likely) that the deaf child treats the written word as though it were ideographic and can go directly from the written word to its referential meaning, bypassing the sound system. This would seem to be an entirely efficient approach. But what happens when the word is entirely unknown? As has been indicated, the verbal labels for objects, events, feelings, and concepts are acquired very gradually, and the meanings that come from the structural and syntactic features of language evolve later for the deaf child than for the hearing child. Learning to read, if it were a matter of using perceptual devices to decode known language, would be different for the deaf child than the hearing child in that visual rather than auditory discrimination would be used, but it would probably be no harder for one than for the other. The problem for deaf children is that at the same time that they are trying to decode the written word they are also trying to learn its meaning; they are treating written language as though it were a primary linguistic activity.

Language Through Reading

To what extent can language be learned initially through reading? Although throughout the years teachers of the deaf have been conducting reading programs that attempt to teach language even more than they teach reading, it is difficult to determine how successful they have been. The written word is the only medium of communication in which the deaf person meets intact language patterns in exactly the same form as anyone else. Therefore, reading would seem to be the ultimate "open sesame" for the deaf, the doorway to the world of language, communication, ideas. And for some few gifted people, reading does indeed function this way. These are the deaf people who somehow, despite their handicap, possess the linguistic awareness that is the *sine qua non* of reading. But the very children whom we would like to salvage through reading (those deaf children who find language hard to acquire through any other medium) experience great trouble with reading. It is possible to build up a vocabulary of word meanings by associating written words directly with the objects or pictures they symbolize. It is even possible to build up comprehension of simple sentence forms, provided they are concrete. But to learn abstract words, and to acquire a sense of what is contributed to meaning by linguistic structure (function words, morphology, syntax) is much more difficult, and would seem to require some language base or talent to begin with. We do not know whether it is at all possible to do this directly through reading, or to what degree it may be possible, or with what kind of learner.

What we do know empirically is that deaf children tend to read the key words in a sentence. If all the key words are known and the sentence structure is simple, the meaning is fairly easily available. If the sentence structure is simple and the meaning concrete (that is, easily converted to referential meaning in terms of object or action) and all but one key word is known, it is possible to learn that new word directly through reading. If, however, the ratio of known to unknown words in the sentence becomes unfavorable (as in my version of "John and His Drum"), it becomes impossible to learn the new words. In other words, to learn new vocabulary—especially abstract words—through reading depends on the preexistence of a fairly high level of linguistic skill. Take your own reading experience as an example. How easy is it for you to figure out the meaning of an entirely new word that you meet for the first time in printed form? Do you generally have to use a dictionary when this happens? And what happens when you meet that word a second time—do you remember its meaning? How many repeated experiences with this word are needed before it really is yours? We may be asking deaf children to do the virtually impossible.

It is important that the teacher of the deaf have a healthy respect for the problems involved in learning to read for someone who has never heard language. It is important because building a reading program for deaf children is a complicated task that takes skill, knowledge, patience, imagination, and a readiness to experiment and explore. Typically, reading lessons with deaf children consist of presenting the children with some kind of written material, which inevitably contains obstacles (in the form of linguistic pitfalls) to comprehension, and then having teacher interpret the reading matter to the children, clarifying the unknown language. I am not suggesting that this reading procedure is wrong or bad or needs to be abandoned entirely. But I do think it should not be the mainstay of reading instruction. The reading program needs to be far more differentiated; the aims more clearly defined; and the activities more varied to meet the needs of children of different linguistic abilities.

As with hearing children, the reading program should provide materials, experiences, and activities for learning to read as well as for reading to learn. The skills taught will be the same, but the materials and activities will have to be adapted to the special needs and problems of the deaf child. Materials for learning to read have to be compatible with the deaf child's actual language level. For the deaf child, reading to learn means two different things. On the one hand, it means what it usually implies—reading to learn about oneself, others, the world about us, past and present, real and imagined. On the other hand, for the deaf child, reading to learn might involve creating a body of written materials designed specifically to systematically teach certain linguistic skills and concepts. I imagine the factor of timing might be important, and that different approaches may profitably be used at different stages of the child's development. For example, some of the linguistic and phonics approaches which make use of the young hearing child's aural knowledge of language may not be suitable for the young deaf child. On the whole, they utilize materials with little intrinsic interest or meaning. But some of these techniques may be beneficial for some older deaf children.

Not that the different facets of the reading program need to be distinctly separated from each other; nor that all materials used need to be adapted and changed. Rather, what is being suggested is that the teacher understand the process of reading for the deaf child so that whatever material or activity is being used, the teacher is clear about what the child can, should be, and is doing, and about how to help the child move along in learning to read, in learning language through reading, and in using reading for personal growth. ☐

2. The reading program

In reading, an invisible author tries to communicate with a reader through a series of visual symbols. The communication is effective when the reader can translate these symbols into referential meanings—an organization of facts, events, characters, and ideas which may be simple and concrete or complicated and abstract, practical and informative or fanciful and imaginative, profound or frivolous, important or trivial, interesting or dull. There is an unlimited quantity and variety of reading materials available, and there are dozens of different ways of reading. We read in different ways and for different purposes depending on the material itself or on our particular need or interest. Looking at a map or a cartoon is reading; noting signs, notices, ads, and labels is reading; following a recipe is reading; skimming a novel is reading; studying a textbook is reading. Sometimes we read because we choose to, and sometimes we read because we have to.

Thus, no single technique or reading system can do the whole job of teaching reading, not for the hearing child and certainly not for the deaf child. Materials and approaches designed for hearing children may be adapted for deaf children, but selectivity is necessary in order to tailor-make a reading program suitable for the individual needs, interests, and abilities of each deaf child. The teacher accumulates and creates specific materials for specific children, using them in different ways for different purposes.

The mechanics of reading are merely the means; the end is to absorb the ideas on the printed page for one's own pleasure or information. Teaching reading is more than teaching a sequence of skills or completing a series of readers; it is leading children to see that reading has meaning and usefulness to them. The emphasis in the reading program should be on reading as an activity, focusing on content; reading lessons that focus on the mechanics are only supplementary. A developmental reading program will present children at successive ages and levels with reading materials of all kinds, developing sequential skills through whichever approaches seem to be appropriate at various stages for various readers.

The Role of the Teacher

Stated briefly, the job of the teacher is to interest children in reading so that they really *want* to read, and to provide them with guided experiences so that they become *able* to read. But this general statement implies a host of complicated skills and knowledges. To motivate, evaluate and diagnose what each child is doing, to provide appropriate materials and set achievable goals, teachers must know a great deal about their children, about the reading process, about materials, programs, and methods. The teacher will find books and courses helpful, but ultimately the best teacher is experience.

Group lessons have some place in a reading program—we all enjoy discussing a book we've read with others who have read it too, and certainly if a story is to be dramatized, group reading can be helpful. But in reality reading is an individual and not a group activity and the best way for the teacher to know where children are at is to observe them individually. Watching the child read can reveal a great deal to a knowledgeable teacher, and having the child sometimes read aloud can reveal even more. The teacher can get a pretty clear idea of the child's interest, attitude, and habits in reading. Is the child restless or bored, checking to see how long the reading selection is? Does the child thumb through the story looking at the pictures first? Is the child's sight vocabulary sufficiently large so that words are quickly and easily recognized? What does the child do about unknown words? How often does the child pause, and why? Is the child's pace so fast, the reading is cursory? Or is it so slow that the beginning is forgotten before the end is reached? How much did the child enjoy what was read? How much and at what level was the material understood?

Checking Comprehension

With deaf children, using written questions to check comprehension is often a self-defeating task. It is using reading to check on reading, and often the child does not understand the language of the question itself. Or, even if the question is understood, the child may not have sufficient expressive language to formulate an answer that will appropriately reflect what he is thinking. The teacher actually has to build into the reading program activities that will systematically and sequentially teach deaf children how to handle written questions.

But there are other ways to glean from the child what impact the story had. Oral questions are easier for deaf children to handle than written questions, and allowing them to answer through words, gestures, actions or pictures will elicit responses that more accurately reveal the quality of the child's reading experience. One of the best techniques for checking comprehension is to engage in dramatic play with the child, acting out selected portions of the story. When children become used to doing this, they automatically transmit to the teacher a great deal of information which will show their grasp and memory for the facts, details, and sequences in the story, their inferences about the characters, highlights, and significant points, as well as their feeling for the general mood or purpose of the story.

Skill Building

The inexperienced teacher may simply be aware that the child has inadequately understood what was read, without knowing precisely what interfered with comprehension, or what to do about it. This teacher then tends to fill in for the child the missed meanings. It may be enjoyable and profitable for the child to have the teacher interpret the story, explaining the new vocabulary and the main ideas, but this alone will not add to the child's ability to read independently the next time.

Experienced teachers are so familiar with all the component skills in reading that as they observe the child read or dramatize a story it is possible for them to pinpoint what is wrong with what the child is doing. To help children develop the needed skills and techniques, teachers can do two things. While the child is reading, the teacher can build in the lacking skill, suggesting or demonstrating a specific word attack approach, for example; or making a comment or asking a question which leads the child to infer or anticipate what may be ahead. Or, the teacher can make a mental note about what the child needs and later provide exercises to promote the specific skill needed. Thus, skill-building exercises should emerge directly from children's actual reading needs. It *is* necessary to isolate a reading skill and provide the child with opportunities to practice and develop the skill. Reading is such a complex process, involving the integration of so many skills, that if one or more things go wrong the entire process may be stalled. It is very helpful, therefore, to create exercises that are controlled so that all factors but the one being worked on are within the child's ability. This gives the child a chance to practice that one skill easily. However, such reading exercises are obviously artificial, and although the child may be able to complete these successfully, the real test of whether the skill has been mastered is whether the child uses the skill not only when it is isolated in an exercise but when it becomes necessary for the child to use that skill in the course of normal reading of more typical reading matter. Too often children are presented with workbooks providing drill in skill sequences. They work through these books, developing great efficiency. However, when they need to use these same skills in "real" reading, they may not recognize it because the format is so different. Skill-building exercises are most effective when they have emerged specifically from the observed needs of the child, and have been designed for that child. After working on a particular skill in isolation, the teacher immediately observes the child to see if that skill is applied in typical reading matter.

What the Reader Does

In the school situation most often the child is given a reading assignment. But normally (both in school and out) the child should be the one doing the selecting. This in itself is a skill, and different children use different bases for choosing—interest in the title or content, pictures or general appearance of the book, personal recommendation, familiarity with the movie or TV version, etc. Presumably, there is greater motivation to read when the choice is the child's own. For the deaf child, particularly, the motivation needs to be strong because the obstacles are great.

To read successfully requires the integration of a host of skills in recognition, comprehension, interpretation, and application. To begin with, it is necessary to decode the printed symbols. This needs to be done fairly quickly. If a word is not recognized quickly on sight, it has to be examined more carefully using various visual and auditory word attack skills (configurational and contextual clues, phonics and word analysis, grammatical clues). With the deaf child, a word that is not recognized is also usually not known; that is, it is not within the child's repertoire of word meanings. To use a dictionary is not only difficult for the deaf child, but slows down reading crucially.

Words need to be recognized quickly because they must be grouped into phrase units within the sentence. For all but the simplest of sentences it is not enough to grasp the lexical meanings; the reader must also recognize and respond to the structural or syntactic meanings. (Standard examples are: *He is easy to please*. vs. *He is eager to please*. *I think of Joe a lot*. vs. *I think a lot of Joe*.) Then, the semantic meaning of each sentence is added to the meaning of each successive sentence until the selection is completed.

At this point the reader should have a literal comprehension of the material read (the sequence of facts, details, events). Mature reading, however, requires going beyond the literal level to achieve inferential comprehension. A government report on reading test results of American schoolchildren defined inferential comprehension as the reader using "the explicit information, along with his personal experiences and thinking abilities, to make predictions, form generalizations, reach conclusions, make comparisons, form judgments and create new ideas." Thus, the quality of a child's reading, how much the child gets from reading, depends not only on specific reading and linguistic skills, but on the depth of experience, knowledge, and thoughtfulness the child brings to the printed word.

Furthermore, whether or not reading can make a meaningful contribution to personal growth depends on what is done with what has been read and understood (at one level or another). Content, whether factual or conceptual, will easily be forgotten unless the reader can analyze the author's intent and message from a very personal point of view—how meaningful or important is it to me? Do I agree with it? Then the reader may store whatever is deemed personally significant deep in some recess of memory, to be retrieved whenever relevant.

If this seems like a formidable compilation of skills and talents, it is. If it seems like an impossible list for deaf children to master, it is for many, but not for all. The teacher's task is to be as knowledgeable as possible, to build the most fitting reading program possible by providing each deaf child with diversified, appropriate reading materials, observing the child's reading habits, and administering skillful help in advancing each child just as far as *that* child can go. The limitations, whatever they are, should be contributed by the child, not by the teacher. The only teacher limitation should be due to the present state of the art. We do not yet know enough to countervail our children's limitations. But we must use all we do know; and we must be willing, courageous and imaginative in experimenting. We must try to see that each and every deaf child acquires minimal skill in reading, and, beyond that, equip children with the skills to read whatever material is relevant to their particular lives.

Facets of the Reading Program

Motivation

A well-balanced reading program should include: motivation, evaluative procedures, a wide variety of rich materials, and a well-organized sequence of reading experiences.

As reading can be a painfully frustrating process for deaf children, it takes tremendous motivation to stick it out. Many will falter and give up, but there will be those who can be inspired, and with patience and determination they will surmount the obstacles. Malcolm X in his autobiography[1] tells the amazing story of how he conquered his illiteracy. He reports that when he first became interested in books while in prison, "...every book I picked up had few sentences which didn't contain anywhere from one to nearly all of the words that might as well have been in Chinese. When I just skipped those words, of course, I really ended up with little idea of what the book said." He set himself to fill in the gaps in his language and vividly described the excitement he experienced when the world of books opened up to him. "I suppose it was inevitable that as my word base broadened, I could for the first time pick up a book and read and now begin to understand what the book was saying. Anyone who has read a great deal can imagine the new world that

[1] Malcolm X., *The Autobiography of Malcolm X.* New York: Ballantine, 1973.

opened. Let me tell you something: from then until I left that prison, in every free moment I had, if I was not reading in the library, I was reading on my bunk. You couldn't have gotten me out of books with a wedge... No university would ask any student to devour literature as I did when this new world opened to me, of being able to read and *understand*."

Most teachers are aware that before introducing a story it is advisable to do something to stimulate the children's interest and curiosity in that particular subject. But it is also important to transmit to children a general appreciation and enthusiasm for the magic carpet of reading, to somehow make them understand that treasures of knowledge and entertainment await them, and miraculous possibilities for transcending time and space are available to them if they enter this wonderful world. The teacher's own attitude and interest in reading are transmitted to children both overtly and covertly. Children readily sense what place reading has in the teacher's life—whether reading is central, whether it is a genuine source of pleasure. The way the teacher conducts storytelling sessions and book discussions, the quality of help extended in reading lessons, all contribute to the aura in which reading is held.

The kinds of books that are available will also affect children's motivation to read. A poorly stocked classroom or library will not represent reading as a favored activity. There should be an abundance of books; the books should be attractive, and they should be attractively displayed. There should be books to meet not only every reading ability level, but every interest, taste, and purpose. If John is especially interested in cats, Jane in fire stations, and Philip has a new baby at home, there should be books about all these subjects. The reading corner should be made as cozy and inviting as possible, with soft cushions and good reading lamps. One teacher created a loft for the reading corner and children climbed up to cuddle up with a book in sublime solitude and comfort. Another teacher hung a decorated sheet over the reading corner creating a tent-like nook as attractive as any circus side show.

Materials

If the goal of the reading program goes beyond achieving respectable scores on reading tests, and is centered on making reading meaningful in the lives of all children at whatever level is appropriate for them, all kind of materials must be used:

1. *Library books of all kinds*—picture books, folk tales, fairy tales, realistic stories, biographies, how-to books, comic books, etc.

2. *Basal readers.* Many schools like to stock one particular series at all levels. The Scott-Foresman Reading Systems, for example, provides within itself a variety of reading experiences.

3. *Supplementary readers.* If one particular basal reader series is used, it is a good idea to supplement it with selected titles from the books in other series to meet special needs. The Bank Street readers, for example, are of special interest to city children; some series provide easy-reading materials (e.g., Pacemaker, Open Highways).

4. *Textbooks.*

5. *Workbooks and skillbuilders.* Some workbooks accompany basal readers; others are independent, such as the Reader's Digest skill texts, the Boning series, the SRA kits, etc.

6. *Magazines and periodicals,* both those published specifically for schoolchildren (such as *My Weekly Reader* and others), and local and national publications.

7. *Reference materials.* Every classroom should have a supply of dictionaries (at the appropriate levels); other materials such as atlases, almanacs and encyclopedia are handy to have in the classroom, but need not necessarily be stocked if the school library provides easy access.

8. *Teacher-made materials.* The number and variety will be as unlimited as the teacher's imagination permits, including stories, charts, worksheets, reference materials, diagrams, signs, etc. This source is a special mainstay in teaching the deaf.

9. *Audio-visual aids*—films, filmstrips, transparencies, slides, etc., vie favorably with TV.

10. *Functional materials*—tags, labels, signs, ads, notices, announcements, posters, recipes, directions on boxes or containers of all kinds, tickets, coupons, catalogs, application forms, rules, etc.

Provision for Success

Another important factor in determining how motivated to read a child will be is the general intellectual liveliness of the child. Children who are passive, who wait to be told what to do, may read out of necessity or conformity, but they rarely become independent readers. On the other hand, children who are inordinately curious and who have lots of active interests will find that books can feed their intellect in both practical and extravagant ways. Thus, a teacher who introduces children to fascinating activities, provides stimulating materials, and prods children to explore and to seek independent sources of nourishment will probably find that these children will value books.

Children, like adults, are easily discouraged by failure and like to do what they do well. Reading is necessarily a very difficult and trying task for deaf youngsters. There is no way that this can be avoided and it is best to face up to it and acknowledge the problem. However, if every attempt at reading is met by frustration and failure, the strongest motivation in the world will not prevail. It is therefore very important that the teacher see to it that pleasurable reading experiences counterbalance the necessarily arduous ones. There are several ways to do this. One way, of course, is to provide materials (commercial or home-made) that children can actually read successfully on their own. This may mean finding easy-reading materials; it may mean rewriting existing materials; it may mean using a ruse such as one I used which turned into a most successful peer tutoring program. Knowing that although the language was appropriate for them, I could not interest 10-year-olds in reading picture books designed for younger children, I asked them instead to help me select picture books for a particular class of younger children. First, we got together with the younger class and paired off. Each older child had to become acquainted with a younger child and discover that child's particular interests. Then we examined library books and each older child chose a book to read to each younger child. We practiced in class and the older children created visual props (paper dolls and other scenic props) to help in getting the story across to the younger child. They became master story tellers, involving and spellbinding their young charges. It was a highly gratifying experience for both classes, and the technique was adopted by other teachers of intermediate and older children.

Another way to demonstrate that reading can be fun is to use materials that are entertaining. The Scholastic Book Services issues many inexpensive books at all levels that are well worth adding to any child's personal library—quiz and riddle books, joke books, cartoon books, puzzle books, poetry, collections of trivia, sports books, etc. Generally, the selections are short, and although the language may not be easy for the deaf child, there may be pictorial and other clues. Besides, the motivation is high enough to make the reward worth the effort.

From my point of view, the most effective way to demonstrate the joys of reading is by reading to children. I don't know a better way to bridge the ability-interest gap. When the teacher reads to children the language level of the material is irrelevant and only the intrinsic interest matters. Children can sit back and relax and thoroughly enjoy a story which they could not read on their own but which is completely appropriate for their age and interests. And the teacher can ham it up in the best thespian tradition. Teachers should choose books they really love in order to transmit their own delight and enthusiasm. I have seen many a class become thoroughly enthralled by such modern classics as *Charlotte's Web*, and I remember one class that could hardly wait for their weekly installment of *Anne of Green Gables*. It is unfortunate that teachers generally stop reading to children beyond the primary level. So far as I'm concerned, no one is too old to enjoy listening to a good story well told.

Evaluation

In order to provide suitable reading materials and to help children develop needed skills and more mature reading habits, some system of evaluating progress is necessary. Standardized tests have some limited usefulness. They are objective and yield quantitative scores, making it possible to measure a child's performance against the norm for that age and to compare progress from year to year. However, standardized tests are a rather poor tool for judging a deaf child's achievement, and it is a pity that there is so much pressure to use them just because they provide easily recordable scores. Designed for the hearing population, these tests are way beyond the language level of deaf children at successive ages and end up being a match and guess game, with children comparing the words in the question with the words in the paragraph to pick one of the answers. (In fact, to raise reading scores it seems to be more effective to teach children how to reduce the possibility of error in guessing than to teach the reading skills presumably being checked on.)

But the major limitation of standardized tests is that they do not yield enough information about the specific habits and deficiencies of the reader, and are not, therefore, very helpful in telling a teacher how to help a child. Diagnostic reading tests also have a limited use with deaf children because they tend to reveal linguistic deficiencies rather than reading problems. They are useful, however, in giving a teacher a listing of the component skills and some idea of the kinds of exercises that might be used for checking out skills sequentially.

Informal testing may not provide quantifiable results, but it will give an experienced and well-organized teacher invaluable information which can be used to design the most appropriate program for each child. Teacher-made exercises and tests have unlimited possibilities in form and content: they may be oral or written, questions, true-false or yes-no statements, completion exercises with or without a choice of answers, matching exercises, etc. The teacher can control the language so that the reading skill itself is focused on (e.g., drawing inferences, relating sub-topics to main topics, organizing ideas, etc.). Because of the problems involved in using questions to check on comprehension with deaf children, there is a tendency to limit such testing to the literal level. It is important to find ways to go further than this and check on what kind of thinking goes along with the child's reading.

Probably the most effective way to check on inferential levels of reading is by teacher observation, during reading sessions as well as at other times. For example, it is easy to note whether and how often a child chooses reading during free-choice times. Does the child bring in books from home or from the neighborhood public library? Does the child bring in information acquired through books? Does the child refer to or use the language or concepts that came up in class reading activities? As was indicated before, having the child read aloud or dramatize a story can provide a wealth of information about the child's reading habits and the depth of her reading experience.

Informal methods of evaluation, in addition to providing more varied and more useful information, have the advantage of retaining the natural reading environment instead of creating an artificial and possibly anxiety-provoking testing situation. The real test of whether skills have been mastered successfully is whether they are applied in real situations. Apart from the fact that informal testing can only be as good as the ingenuity of the teacher makes it, the chief drawback of such evaluative techniques is that, not being quantifiable, the results often remain in the teacher's head and are never recorded. Teachers should try to get into the habit of keeping running notes on each child, recording specific observations. These will help enormously in the selection of materials and in the design of remedial exercises for each child. The amalgamation of all these notes will also help in designing the overall program; they will indicate to the teacher how to use different materials in different ways for different purposes, when to work individually and when to work in a group, when to read to children and when to have them read to the teacher or to each other, when to allow children to read with minimum or no checking and when to check thoroughly, when to use reading for language growth, and how to promote reading through language work.

Components of the Reading Program

Reading instruction is not limited to one period in the school day; reading goes on all day long in relation to all school subjects and activities. In *all* reading the child's *sight vocabulary, word attack skills*, and *comprehension skills* are being developed. In addition, to ensure that there is systematic instruction and evaluation, some specific time is set aside each day when reading is the designated activity. It is for this time that the reading teacher needs to plan. Supervised and unsupervised reading will take place at many other times during the day, and during these times teachers should be seeing that the children are using and improving the skills developed in the reading period.

For purposes of clarification, it may be helpful to the teacher to differentiate reading experiences into developmental, functional, remedial, and recreational activities. Because teaching reading to the deaf is so difficult and complex, this kind of breakdown may help to clarify the relationship between language and reading and may reassure the teacher that it is possible both to separate and integrate the teaching of reading and the teaching of language through reading.

Developmental Reading (Reading Known Language)

Developmental reading consists of guided reading sessions designed to systematically develop and promote sequential skills in reading. For this purpose the most commonly used materials for hearing children are basal readers because they provide a gradual progression from easy to more difficult levels. Furthermore, the workbooks and teachers' guidebooks accompanying basal readers contain many helpful suggestions by reading experts. Of course, there are those teachers who favor a basal reader because group reading lessons are facilitated when many children can use the same book at the same time.

If the teacher accepts as a basic criterion for selection of reading materials their intrinsic interest to children, it can be seen that the considerations above have more to do with teacher comfort than with child needs. Philosophical considerations apart, however, it is debatable how useful a basal reader series actually is for the deaf child. As controlled as they may be, the vocabulary and sentence structure of basal readers are still beyond the language level of the deaf child at each successive age level. Many basal reader series have attractively illustrated stories, and many publishers have begun packaging individual stories in paperback, making them eminently usable with deaf children. But so are trade books, library books, children's newspapers, filmstrips, and so on. I am suggesting that any and all of these sources should be used for developmental reading, and that the teacher should select those materials which seem to offer the greatest promise in motivating children to want to read.

The important thing is what is done with what has been chosen for developmental reading. The purpose, as has been noted, is to present to the child enticing reading material and to observe and guide the child in the reading so as to strengthen that child's growing skill in reading. Ideally, developmental reading is conducted with material where the language is completely known to the child so that there is no interference with the child's developing more and more mature habits and skills in reading. This virtually prohibits the use of commercial materials for these purposes for the deaf child, since none of these keep pace with his slower linguistic development. And, in reality, I would say that the best way to promote sequential reading skills for deaf children is through the use of special teacher-made materials, where the language is designed to be within the child's ability, and reading techniques can be worked on unadulterated by language deficiencies. Traditionally, over the many years, teachers of the deaf have created their own stories for teaching reading. However, it would be as short-sighted to limit deaf children's developmental reading to teacher-made materials as it would be to limit it to basal readers, or any other one source. As charming as the productions of teachers may be, they are not "the real thing." And apart from not wanting to deprive deaf children of the joy of handling "real" books, we do not know how much carry-over there is from spoon-feeding to self-feeding. Thus, while teacher-made stories should play a fundamental role in developmental reading, they should not be used to the exclusion of other materials.

Now, with the use of commercial materials (whether they be basal readers, library books, comic books, newspapers, or what have you), we face the problem of how to promote sequential reading skills when language difficulties interfere. Unfortunately there is no simple solution. My answer may seem disingenuous, but I feel the child cannot be burdened with this overwhelming problem, and that it can only be sorted out and coped with in the mind of the teacher. To begin with, I think it is helpful to make two distinctions. One is the difference between reading failure that can be traced to deficiencies in language, versus defective reading techniques. If we define developmental reading as the development of sequential skills in reading *known* language, then failure due to language deficiencies must be ruled out. A second distinction is to be made between learning new language through reading and teaching new language through reading. In the former, the burden of responsibility is on the child, in the latter on the teacher. All deaf children can be taught new language through reading; reading, along with every other activity the child is involved in, is the source for guided language growth. But only some deaf children (those gifted with linguistic ability which emerges despite their deafness) will be able to learn new language independently through reading. For these children reading will indeed be the major avenue for linguistic growth as well as for all other intellectual growth. But even these children cannot learn new language through reading until they have a minimal linguistic base.

In other words, all deaf children need the opportunity to develop reading skills in sequence unencumbered by the need to learn new language concepts at the same time. Since most reading material (except that specifically created by the teacher) does not allow for this, the adjustment has to be made by the teacher. That is, the teacher has to observe specifically whether the difficulty a child is having is due to a language deficiency or to a poor reading technique. If it is due to a language deficiency the teacher should immediately remove this obstacle by explaining the word or construction, freeing the child to use reading skills to decode the sentence meaning. The teacher makes a note of the unknown vocabulary item or linguistic construction and subsequently teaches this new form through language activities or through remedial reading activities. Meanwhile, the child has had a chance to exercise appropriate reading skills with minimal interference from linguistic stumbling blocks.

It is not necessary or advisable for the teacher to stop a reading lesson in order to teach needed language. A brief explanation and a jotting down of the linguistic items are called for in order to allow the child to get on with the reading. But if reading is to be the source of language growth, recording the linguistic obstacles and follow-up activities teaching and reinforcing the new forms are essential.

In other words, in developmental reading the teacher guides the child to use appropriate reading skills to independently figure out the meaning of known language. Whenever unknown language interferes with this process, the teacher takes steps to remove this obstacle, either by pre-teaching the unknown linguistic forms, or by freely explaining them during the reading and teaching them in depth afterwards. Just a word here about pre-teaching: putting a list of new words and their definitions on the board or on paper just before the reading is not really pre-teaching. It would be better to follow the suggestion of waiting to interpret the new language until the child is in the middle of the reading, where contextual clues will aid immeasurably in understanding the new terms. If the teacher really intends to pre-teach the vocabulary and language of the story, it takes more than listing and defining. The new linguistic forms have to be incorporated into language activities where they will be associated with events, actions, ideas which will fix them in the child's language repertoire so that they will be remembered and retrieved when the child encounters these terms in reading. Just exposing the child to the new language just before the reading session, and requiring the child to remember and apply the new terms immediately is asking too much.

It is clear that just as language and reading go hand in hand, developmental and remedial reading go hand in hand. The process may be laborious, but it's like building a house brick by brick, with complete satisfaction delayed until the whole work is finished.

Remedial Reading (Teaching Language Through Reading)

Generally, remedial reading for the deaf child does not involve teaching reading skills as such, but is directed at ameliorating specific language deficiencies. In other words, this is where using reading to promote language comes in. Remedial reading activities can take two different forms. As has been indicated, in guiding the child through developmental reading activities, the teacher notes the semantic and syntactic forms that were unknown. Having provided as much of an explanation of these forms as was needed to enable the child to proceed with the reading, the teacher later returns to these forms to teach them more thoroughly. They will be entered into the various vocabulary books or other systems used by the class to keep track of new language, and the teacher will construct games, exercises and tests for further drill in the understanding and use of these linguistic forms. Finally, the teacher will be alert for every opportunity for natural use of these forms in real activities and experiences.

Remedial reading may also be independent of other reading materials and activities. It is here that much experimentation can be attempted to see whether, how, to what extent, and to whom, language may be initially taught through reading. Systematic programs to teach aspects of vocabulary (synonyms, antonyms, idioms, multiple meanings, figures of speech, etc.), morphology (plurals, verb forms, etc.), and syntax (clauses, question forms, etc.) may be devised and tested with different children.

Of course there is still another purpose for remedial reading, which is to provide drill in specific reading skills. Children who need more practice than is provided in developmental reading may benefit from special remedial exercises in order to master the decoding of known language. Usually, however, these children have handicaps over and above deafness that interfere with their visual as well as auditory perception. These are the children who, unfortunately, fail to acquire even minimum linguistic skill. It certainly is worthwhile to do whatever is possible to enable them to read material that interests them at whatever level they can achieve.

Functional Reading (Reading as a Means to an End)

Developmental and remedial reading relate to reading instruction and usually involve special reading materials. Functional and recreational reading, on the other hand, represent reading in its natural form and require no special materials, beyond a teacher fully alert to the potential for promoting children's desire and ability to read.

In functional reading, reading is not the primary activity; there is a task at hand which necessitates reading for its completion. For example, you may be reading a recipe in order to bake a cake, or following directions for knitting, or looking up the TV schedule to see what's on that night, or reading the label in a sweater to find out if it can be washed, etc. Every parent who has had a preschool-age child identify a favorite product on the shelves in the supermarket is impressed with how effectively TV commercials promote not only their products but functional reading. Although functional reading is virtually unavoidable, we sometimes fail to take full advantage of all the opportunities that exist. There are countless occasions for functional reading—following directions for a new game, putting together an unassembled toy, comparing weights and prices on boxes of cookies, looking up the breed of Billy's new dog, etc.—all such activities demonstrate to children the important uses of reading in their lives. The teacher of the deaf will generally find that the language in functional reading, while often technical and requiring much drill and repetition (baste, simmer, diagonally, upper left hand corner, every other, etc.), is concrete and easily converted into visible referential meaning.

Recreational Reading (Reading for Pleasure and Information)

Most reading activities are arduous affairs for deaf children. It is therefore terribly important to make sure that the reading program includes time for reading without struggling mightily, reading without someone "breathing down your neck" to check your level of comprehension. If adults had to take a test on every book we read, we might soon be discouraged from reading. Children should be given daily opportunities to read whatever material they choose, for whatever purpose they set for themselves, in whatever way and at whatever level of comprehension they are capable of, without adult interference or guidance. They should have access to good libraries in class, in school, and in their home communities. Skilled librarians who know children's literature can do a great deal to stimulate children's interest in books. (They can, of course, also work with the teacher in promoting the skills of developmental reading.) Attractive book displays, talks with authors, and storytelling sessions all help to make reading an enjoyable experience. The goal of any reading program is to cultivate the *habit* of reading; outside the school world this means recreational reading.

The activities which follow in this monograph present a sequential program for the teaching of reading to the deaf. They have been assembled from the programs and resources used to teach reading to children with normal hearing, and have been adapted to take into account the pace and special problems of deaf children. If this manual is to be of help, it must be used as a guide and not as a blueprint. Although containing a wide variety of practical suggestions, it is in no way exhaustive. The activities are intended to be illustrative; resourceful teachers will expand on these and improvise others. This book presents no final solutions to the problems of reading for the deaf. It simply describes an approach and a program. Many problems remain. We await further research and experimentation to resolve some of these problems in order to make reading the medium for breakthrough in enabling deaf children to utilize their full potential.

3. Preschool

The preschool level, embracing the first five-and-a-half years of life, describes what happens during a child's earliest years, whether in school or at home. Fortunately, infant programs and nursery and kindergarten programs are recognized as being necessary and valuable for the deaf child, and such programs are even more prevalent for deaf children than they are for hearing children. It is not only the deaf child, but also the parents of the deaf child, who need specialized help from experts as early as possible. Thus, most deaf children are likely to be attending school on some basis during this period of their lives.

As reading instruction does not begin generally until the child is about 6, why should preschool be included in a book on the teaching of reading? If we think about what we can build into children's environments from the day they are born that will make them grow up to be eager, competent readers, we will agree that the groundwork for later success can be laid in the cradle. Since reading is a language-based activity, and the early years are the critical ones in terms of language learning, the importance of the preschool years in relation to reading becomes obvious. For the deaf child, in particular, this is true. We cannot afford to let these crucial years go by without maximally using them for linguistic growth.

The reading program at the preschool level is generally termed "reading readiness" to distinguish it from formal reading. Usually at this level the child is not taught or held responsible for interpreting the printed word, but is exposed to a program of vital experiences and activities that will promote linguistic, perceptual, and conceptual skills that will ultimately be applied to reading. In other words, the preschool program makes the child ready to read.

The readiness concept is a very important one, and has meaning that extends far beyond the reading program at the preschool. Readiness exists not only for reading but for almost any form of human activity—not just during the first years, but throughout life. Readiness determines the depth of human experience in relation to any activity. (For example: If you reread Shakespeare's *Julius Caesar* as an adult, you would get something completely different from it than you did reading it in high school. If you visited a foreign country as an adult you might see it entirely differently from the way you saw it if you were taken there by your parents when you were younger.) The readiness principle implies that there is an optimum time in the life of the individual for the development of a new insight or skill. Introducing it prematurely will, at best, constitute a waste of time and effort. At worst, it will create antagonistic reactions which may retard rather than accelerate growth. The question of timing is therefore very important, and the teacher must be alert to the signals. To pick these up, the teacher must know about the development of children in general, about where any one child is in particular, and about the component skills that go into whatever is being taught (in this case, reading).

Many factors combine to determine readiness; some of them are maturational and some are experiential. Thus, determining readiness is a two-fold process of observing children's physical, social, and intellectual development, and of providing appropriate materials, activities, and experiences to promote their growth. To know when and what kind of experiences to introduce to specific children, the teacher should observe their general state of health, motor coordination, pace, degrees of independence, confidence, and initiative, their special interests, likes and dislikes, curiosity, memory and attention span, frustration tolerance, creativity, organizing and problem-solving abilities, linguistic awareness, comprehension and use of language.

There are skills such as visual and auditory discrimination, part-whole relationships, etc., that relate specifically to reading.

These may be promoted through all the usual preschool activities if the teacher is aware of them. Or, they may be developed through special exercises and drills such as those in reading readiness workbooks. The teacher will have to make the judgments as to when, how, and why to use such materials for each child individually. A particular child may benefit more from sorting seashells or going to the zoo than from completing a worksheet, while another child may need and profit from special drill. A long time ago, I was a camp counselor with a group of 4-year-olds which included one profoundly deaf child. When the laundry came back each week, it was the deaf child who did all the sorting for me. She not only matched up pairs of socks, but also sorted out which socks, pants, and shirts belonged to whom. This child did not need the visual discrimination exercises in reading readiness workbooks. The program should be flexible enough, and the teacher perceptive and knowledgeable enough, to provide children with what they need most at a particular time. The important thing is to recognize what children actually need, and not to impose on them those things that are in a curriculum outline, or that symbolize growth to adults.

Should Formal Reading be Taught?

There is a strong and understandable urge to introduce formal reading very early to the deaf child in order to promote language growth. Hearing children automatically learn language every minute of their waking days simply because their ears are unstopped. The input to the deaf child, by contrast, is infinitesimal, and the burden of trying to perceive language visually instead of casually taking it in auditorily is overwhelming. The only time deaf children receive language is when they are deliberately exposed to it and are attending. Hearing children not only hear language all day long, they overhear it. This means that in addition to hearing language addressed to them at the child level, they are overhearing language at the adult level not intended for them. Deaf children will learn only what language they are taught. This places a staggering responsibility on teachers of the deaf, who have to decide what to teach, how to teach it, and when to teach it. It would be nice if deaf children could be readers so that they could supplement their limited language intake through reading. This is a goal "devoutly to be wished," but, as has been indicated, the problems are massive.

The question of when to begin to teach formal reading involves deciding when, in view of the limited time available, deaf children can profit more from reading instruction than from other kinds of teaching experiences. The answer probably should not be made for deaf children in general, but for each child in particular, with that child's needs and abilities in mind. Nevertheless, I am inclined to feel that formal reading should not be introduced at the preschool level, certainly not across the board, routinely.

Reading is a linguistic function, and usually children understand and use spoken language before they understand and use written language. It is quite clear that whereas most normal youngsters find it relatively easy to learn to talk, a great many of them do not find it so easy to learn to read. How can we expect the reverse to be true of deaf children? How can we expect them to learn written language before and more easily than they learn spoken language? Learning to read is a highly complex human act requiring motivation and an array of perceptual skills (detecting likenesses and differences and perceiving distinctive features and patterns in phonemes, word roots, and affixes, etc.). Comprehension requires an ability to relate linguistic symbols to referential meanings. This assumes a wide vocabulary of both common and uncommon words and an ability to react to syntactic arrangements. Comprehension also involves conceptual skills (ordination and subordination, the ability to build from details into broader meanings, the ability to organize and generalize, to make inferences, and to draw conclusions, etc.). Comprehension not only depends on linguistic, thinking, and abstracting skills; it is also crucially affected by the extent to which one can bring to bear past experience and knowledge. Memory, the ability to store items for later use, is also involved.

Can this impressive assortment of competencies be introduced to the preschooler? Jerome Bruner says, ". . . the foundations of any subject may be taught to anybody at any age in some form" (Bruner, 1960). While I am less than eager to teach formal reading at the preschool level, I am very enthusiastic about developing perceptual, linguistic, and thinking skills in very young deaf children—in fact, the younger the better. I regard these as being the foundations for reading.

I have no doubt that young deaf children can be taught to recognize words in print. But I wonder: Would this be worthwhile? Would learning to read at an earlier age accelerate language learning? Would gains be maintained and enlarged? From what I have seen of formal attempts to teach reading to the young deaf child, I am inclined to believe that for most children there is no appreciable benefit to be gained. The words that young deaf children can be taught to read are concrete words which name the objects and visible things in the environment. I do not feel that this effectively promotes language skills; they will learn to read these words more easily and quickly later on. What they might have difficulty with later on is syntactic meaning. It would be better to try to build this up from the start. If the time spent teaching formal reading to deaf children limits the time available for exposing them to meaningful and varied language forms, it will not be worth it in the long run. There are more beneficial ways of using young deaf children's learning time—ways that promote broad language comprehension, enhance their experiential and conceptual background, and give them self-confidence to develop their own interests and thinking skills. Later on, children who have spent their early school years building a good language foundation will be able to apply this knowledge of language and meaning to the printed page with success. Still later on, they can use reading to expand their language. But there must first be a foundation upon which to build. The best preparation for reading we can give to deaf children is to improve their vocabulary and ability to understand different sentence structures by using language in relation to all their on-going experiences. Reading exercises contrived to develop specific sequences of language cannot tap the actual language experiences or meet the actual language needs of the child. Young deaf children experience the world visually. Language has little or no place in this world. The best way to make language meaningful is to relate it directly to children's experiences, feelings, and needs. Drills and exercises, whether spoken or written, rarely do this.

Nevertheless, there are some preschoolers who should be taught reading. Obviously, those who tell you in various ways that they are ready should not be held back. These children may love storytelling sessions and remember the stories; they choose to look at books during free choice time; they start writing on their own. They should be encouraged to read.

It may also be worthwhile to try to reach, through reading, children who seem not to respond to language in any other way. But even with such children I can't see how written language drills could help. I think what I'd do with nonverbal children, in addition to giving them lots of direct experiences, is to write simple little one- and two-page booklets all about them. Rather than having them memorize isolated written words, I would try to make language meaningful to them through strong personal appeal. I would draw pictures of the individual children and their possessions and activities and use these as the bases for writing captions and simple stories in which they starred.

While the preschool program needs to be differentiated to meet the needs of individual children, reading is best promoted at this level through the procedures and activities that are standard in good preschool practice. These have to do with giving children direct experiences in exploring their home, school, and neighborhood environments; encouraging children to experiment, compare, question, create; and giving children something to think about and talk about.

The Written Word in the Preschool

Although I do not look kindly on the formal teaching of reading to very young deaf children, I am not opposed to using the printed word at the preschool level. I would heartily encourage the functional use of reading and writing in relation to the children's experiences and activities. This does not mean flooding the classroom with writing; it means using the printed word in ways that are very natural and intrinsic to the activity. For example, labeling everything in the room is not functional (and probably would not teach children these words because they are not relevant, and a superfluity would tend to be ignored). However, putting labels on things which need to be distinguished so that they can be used more effectively is an excellent use of reading. You can label children's cubbies and clothes, for example, or put their names on their creative productions, label boxes of supplies (crayons, scissors, paper, paint, etc.), or call attention to the labels on food boxes , toys, street signs, and so on. Written language can also be used to enhance other class activities; for example, writing captions for pictures taken on a school trip; recording observations for scientific experiments *(We watered this plant. We did not water this plant. The magnet picked these things up. The magnet did not pick these things up.),* following recipes, writing thank you notes, etc. This kind of reading and writing is functional; it not only promotes the language of the activity, but also gives children a sense of usefulness of reading.

Aims

Since the major aim during the preschool years is to lay a foundation which will assure the greatest possible success in reading later on, the activities which do this may be thought of in these three ways:

1. <u>Those which promote social, emotional, and cognitive growth.</u>

Studies conducted by the Pre-School Project of Harvard indicate that there is a relationship between the child's activity level—curiosity, drive to explore—and the amount of stimulation in the environment. The amount of purposeless behavior—sitting and doing nothing, or moving about aimlessly—was much higher in environmentally impoverished homes, and the amount of exploratory activity—especially role-play and pretend activity—was higher where there were interesting things to interact with in the environment. The preschool teacher has to provide an atmosphere in which children are encouraged to observe, experiment, explore, reason, and imagine. The teacher has to provide materials and equipment of all kinds, and a program of individual and group activities in and outside the classroom that will promote concepts about the self and about the physical and social world.

2. <u>Those which promote linguistic awareness.</u>

We know that the first five years of life are the important ones in terms of language growth. We do not know what limitations to linguistic development may accrue if optimal use is not made of this ideal learning time. From studies of growth, Benjamin S. Bloom concludes that environmental factors have a maximum impact on a developing characteristic during the stage of most rapid growth for that characteristic. Human intelligence and language develop most rapidly during the first five years, so this is the time when the child can most effectively learn the language of all the objects, activities, and experiences in the immediate environment. It takes skill on the part of the teacher to see that the language of the activity is made meaningful to the deaf child and is the source of verbal as well as non-verbal growth.

3. <u>Those which promote specific reading readiness skills.</u>

Without holding the child responsible for a specific reading vocabulary, the teacher can cultivate in the child certain attitudes and skills in relation to reading. Prime and foremost is the nurturing of an interest and love of books. Next is the awareness of the existence and purpose of the written word. Using reading functionally usually not only accomplishes this, but also results in the child's casually acquiring some meaningful sight words (first on this list is usually the child's own name). Other reading skills which are developed (primarily through pictures rather than words) at this level are: an awareness of sequence, visual and some auditory discrimination skills, hand-eye coordination, and the habit of left-to-right eye movement across a line of pictures, symbols, or words.

Although I have divided the activities into three distinct categories, I certainly am not suggesting that the goals are worked on independently. There are times when they are, but most often they overlap heavily, and any one activity contributes to growth in various areas, especially under the guidance of an alert, skillful teacher. It is important to repeat that how successfully children read will depend on their linguistic skill and on the quality of thinking and personal experience they bring to the written word. These are what are being promoted through all the varied preschool activities.

The Classroom

When children enter the preschool department they have their first experience with SCHOOL. What they encounter, and its impact on them, will be of great importance in the formulation of their habits, attitudes, and values. Young children leaving home for the first time are on the brink of a momentous experience. They come into an environment which, in all its strangeness, is both appealing and frightening. They will want to explore this environment, but they need to feel safe. If the atmosphere minimizes fear, they will wander freely, create, and learn. Children will learn what school is all about, and what is expected of them from the looks of the classroom, from the way the day's activities are organized, and from the verbal and non-verbal behavior of the teacher. The teacher is the vital force in establishing the atmosphere. The children will learn what is central—the children themselves, their behavior, or their achievement; they will learn what gives the teacher joy and what distresses the teacher; and they will learn what brings them approval or disapproval. They will learn what is valued in school; they will learn how free they are and what limits they must observe; they will learn what input they themselves can have on what happens to them in school and whether school really meets their needs; they will learn whether they can be happy in school.

The teacher of the deaf has an even greater obligation to children. Not only must their needs as children be met, but also their needs as deaf children. In making the adjustments required by the deafness, it is altogether possible to ignore and even violate the normal needs of children. Because the world offers them fewer clues, deaf children may be even more frightened by school than hearing children. Teachers of the deaf should recognize that young deaf children, like young hearing children, need to feel safe, loved, and understood before they can interact meaningfully to the environment. Many a teacher, misled into believing that the deaf child's lack of language is the chief problem, exposes children to language lessons prematurely, thus burdening their young lives with still another puzzling task. Pintner has said, "It has often seemed to me that we have been trying to teach the young deaf child words and phrases before he has had enough experience with the underlying reality, and furthermore we use too much valuable time in early schooling on drill in speech and lipreading, time which might more profitably be spent in real living" (Pintner, Eisenson, & Stanton, 1945, p. 179).

This in no way implies that the deaf child is not in dire need of language. It is a question of timing and approach. If instead of being given drill in language, speech, and reading, deaf children are encouraged to participate actively in the events and activities of school life, they will in fact learn language, speech, and reading. They may even master these skills more rapidly—if only because these skills will have more meaning to them if they grow out of their own direct experiences. The teacher who patiently creates a living, loving classroom will be rewarded by happy, learning children. The classroom environment should be attractive, comfortable, and orderly. It should stimulate interests and ideas. There should be colorful and carefully selected pictures, signs, and posters, all kinds of play equipment and books. The equipment should allow for active play and quiet play. There should be provision for creative outlets of all kinds. There should be areas where children can run and jump and make noise. There should be areas where children can sit and play quietly. There should be nooks where a child can go to be alone.

Play equipment should include blocks, bicycles, slides, wagons, and swings to develop big muscle coordination, as well as puzzles, paints, cut-outs, clay, etc., to develop coordination of small muscles and manual skills. There should be a well-equipped doll corner with all kinds of furniture, and clothes to pretend in. There should be opportunities for water play, and for play in a sand box. There should be noise makers and music makers, records, a record player, a tape recorder and a TV. The equipment should be placed attractively in the room. At the same time, separation between work and play areas should be provided so that children are not constantly interfering with one another.

What the Child Does

Surrounded by this wealth of materials and equipment, what is the child to do? The answer is simple—play. It is through play that the child explores the world and begins to give that world size, shape, values, and meaning.

It has aptly been said, "Play is not simply play. It is the young child's work, his education. Through it children unconsciously learn to adapt to life and take an active part in it. They play out human relations; they discover how to live with others; they learn more about themselves and their role in relation to other people. They begin to clarify the role of men and women in their communities. They develop control over inanimate objects and learn the relationships, qualities and uses of these and how to get results they conceive for themselves. In play they set their own standards and measure themselves with their own yardsticks of success... Through play they begin to clarify confusions, orient themselves to their immediate world, solve problems and build concepts, the basis for later academic achievement in school" (New York State Education Department, 1955, p. 75).

The child's play takes a variety of forms including indoor play and outdoor play, quiet play and active play, solitary play and play with others, creative play, physical play, intellectual play, dramatic play, competitive play, and cooperative play. The teacher who has observed how utterly absorbed a child becomes in play activity comes to recognize that this type of concentration is exactly what is desired in "work" tasks. The teacher begins to have respect for the nature and results of play, and relinquishes the typical adult's suspicion of play as compared with work.

I am reminded of a parent who was watching a group of 6-year-olds working diligently to master horse-reining. Her unspoken attitude was, "This is all well and good, but when do they get down to the more serious business of learning?" When the parent was told that the activity was part of a project on what things are made of (the children had observed things being made of wood in the carpentry shop and were now making potholders woven of yarn), and that it also was helping them develop the fine motor coordination that is needed for learning to write, her attitude of barely tolerating a play activity changed to one of respect. Sometimes adults need training and experience to appreciate and spot the specific things children learn through play.

The Program

Although the days are dominated by play, they take on form and continuity based on children's physical needs, as well as on their growing social and intellectual interests. There is much diversity as well as much repetition of patterns.

A typical day at this level might unfold as follows: The children arrive one by one, are greeted, hang up their clothing in their own cubbies. They choose some toy or activity during a period designated in the adult mind as "free play." A child may choose a bicycle or a wagon, a puzzle or a book, some clay or paint, blocks, a doll, or some dress-up clothes. The teacher circulates about the room chatting with different children, offering help when it is needed, providing needed supplies, settling an argument, hanging a child's drawing on the wall. She instantly uses language appropriate to whatever is going on and is constantly alert to the functional use of reading in pointing out relevant signs, labeling a picture, making a chart (a good way to stop a fight over who may use a favorite toy or material in limited supply).

If the weather permits, the group may go outdoors to swings and jungle gym, bicycles, slides, and sand box. Soon it is time to come in, wash, go to the bathroom and enjoy a mid-morning snack. Next may come a finger-play or storytelling session. The rest of the morning may be spent taking a short excursion into the community, to the local pet shop to buy food for the fish, to the zoo, down to the river to see the boats, to the store to buy seeds, or to the park to collect leaves. Or, the children may stay in to make something—Jello or popcorn, papier-mache decorations, a potholder, or boats out of milk cartons. Just before lunch there is a quiet group activity, probably a "song" or imitative game, followed by a nap. When they get up, the children may choose any toy or activity; or the teacher may have a game, a film strip or rhythm band instruments ready for those who want to participate. After a busy day it is time to put on hats and coats and go home.

As the school year progresses from September to June, there is much room for variation as seasonal, holiday, and science activities are introduced. Materials become more challenging, picture puzzles more intricate, books more meaty. Planned activities are enriched in conceptual content, and the participation of the children becomes more mature and meaningful. Group activities may become more frequent as youngsters find experiments with water, light, and other science and social science areas fascinating. Trips within and outside the school also form the concrete, directly experiential basis for abstract concepts. Even free play activities show growth. Concepts from group activities are carried over into the child's play with blocks and doll. The children spontaneously use the souvenirs and props accumulated on field trips, and, hopefully, the language. Outdoor play begins to include such organized games as "Bluebird," "London Bridge," etc.

Through all these activities and under the encouraging guidance of understanding adults, the young deaf child evolves from a passive observer of a silent, confusing scene to an active participant—exploring, seeking, and gaining meaningful interactions.

Having arrived at school with no understanding of language or even any awareness of its existence, the child slowly begins to recognize its function and usefulness. As language is used over and over again in association with all the immediate activities, deaf children begin to get some idea of how language functions. If they discover that they can more quickly satisfy their wants through the use of language, then language comes to have a purpose in their lives. Language begins to be seen as the miraculous tool it really is if they see, for example, how much more effective it is to name a desired toy or a needed supply than to try to drag a busy teacher over to a cabinet where it is locked up; or, if asking for *two* cookies acquires them whereas grabbing them brings gentle but firm disapproval.

Exposing young deaf children to drill in language sequences which have no immediate relevance to their lives is fairly meaningless to them. If the teacher uses language in everyday situations which clearly establish the meaning of the words, the children will get all the practice and repetition they need to learn the words, and they will get a definite sense of the usefulness of language in communicating ideas. Because they are based on children's actual interests and choices, the activities in preschool (individual and group) give children opportunities for developing everyday vocabulary (e.g., names of all the toys, foods, clothing), abstract terms (more, fast, animal), and conversational language (*Let me see, I don't have that, I want a ball*). By the end of preschool most deaf children are used to understanding ideas through spoken language and use words and phrases interspersed with gestures to make their own ideas known. They have begun to build the language foundation necessary for reading.

Reading Activities

All the activities of the preschool promote reading generally, in building linguistic and cognitive abilities, and specifically, in providing functional, recreational and skill-building reading experiences.

The functional use of reading and writing pins down some of the concepts, language, and sequences of experience. It thus promotes memory and gives children a specific awareness of written symbols. Concrete concepts about observable data as well as abstract ideas about size, shape, function, order, class, relation, and causality may be promoted through the judicious use of functional reading. Some examples follow.

1. It is likely that the first words children learn to read are their own and their classmates' names. They learn to recognize names by repeatedly seeing them on labels on their possessions, on their art work, and on duty and health charts, etc.

I FEED THE FISH	
MON.	John
TUES.	Susan
WED.	Marty
THURS.	Bob
FRI.	Ann

	Monday			Tuesday			Wednesday			Thursday			Friday		
	Nails	Teeth	Hair	Nails	Teeth	Hair	Nails	Teeth	Hair	Nails	Teeth	Hair	Nails	Teeth	Hair
• Ann															
Bob																
John																
Marty																
Susan																

2. Some of the tools and equipment in the room may be labeled. These labels should be functional; boxes containing objects and supplies that are needed by the children should be tagged (e.g., paste, scissors).

3. Attention may be called to meaningful signs as they are encountered (e.g., teachers' names on doors, traffic signs, store signs, names on candy wrappers and food containers, etc.).

Bulletin board announcements and posters may be used. Some should be simple and appropriate commercial ones (e.g., safety posters with a simple "Stop, Look and Listen" text) to introduce "real" reading materials, and some should be teacher-made (e.g., a caption "Spring is here" mounted over children's drawings).

One nursery teacher brought in a particularly beautiful sea shell. He put it in a box and placed a sign over it which simply said,

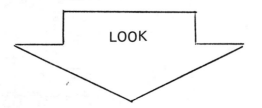

LOOK

His children were encouraged in this simple, dramatic way to pay attention to printed symbols.

In a certain nursery, each time the teacher took her children outdoors she put a notice on the door, "We're in the yard." Her children, observing this routine, soon came to her before they went out and asked for the notice for the door. They couldn't read the words, but they knew that the sign told everyone where they were.

Many preschool teachers hang on their doors a pie chart which can be rotated so that the revealed section gives information about where the class may be found.

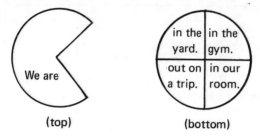

(top)   (bottom)

4. Simple written charts may be used in morning calendar, weather, and attendance discussions. Children complete the sentences by using picture clues and matching.

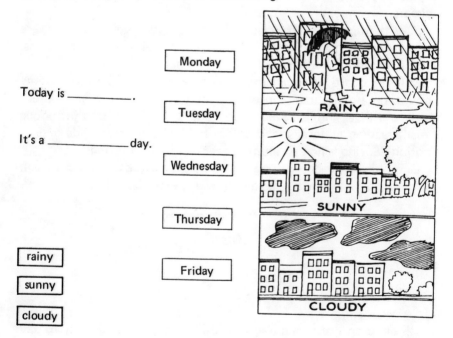

The attendance chart can consist of pictures of the individual children inserted into slots. At the end of the day, the teacher turns them face down. In the morning, as children's names are called, they turn them face up. Then they count.

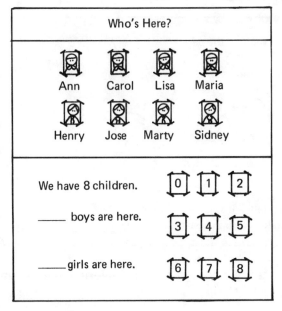

5. The happenings and results of experiences in and outside school may be recorded simply on charts illustrated with pictures (drawn by the children or cut out of magazines) or with "found" objects. Or a camera may be used during the activity; later the children can arrange the pictures in sequence and make a book. The teacher may write a brief caption under each picture.

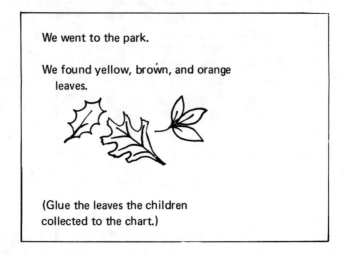

We went to the park.

We found yellow, brown, and orange
   leaves.

(Glue the leaves the children
collected to the chart.)

Each page has a photograph taken during the activity, and a sentence written by the teacher later.

Making Jello	*Photograph* Mary got a bowl.	*Photograph* Henry got a cup.

Photograph Ruth put the Jello in the bowl.	*Photograph* Michael put a cup of water in the bowl.	*Photograph* Andrea put a cup of water in the bowl, too.

Photograph Sarah mixed.	*Photograph* Howie mixed, too.	*Photograph* Mrs. B. put the bowl in the refrigerator.

Photograph

We all ate the Jello. Mmmm!
It was good.

Storytelling

If I were asked what I think is the most important thing a parent or teacher can do to promote reading in the preschool, I would say *read to the child*. Hearing children who are read to a great deal and who know their favorite stories by heart generally turn out to be early and good independent readers. Gates (1942) has written that in judging reading readiness, "most important for diagnostic purposes is the ability to grasp and enjoy the substance of a story—the main ideas, the plot, the organization, the probable next steps in, or outcome. In our most extensive investigation it was found that this ability to grasp the structure and substance of a story gave one of the highest correlations with later progress in reading."

Many adults shy away from reading to deaf children because they don't know how to go about it and because they don't think it will mean very much or be very enjoyable to the deaf child. But with a little experience, you will find it's not so hard to release the "ham" in you. And it is an extremely worthwhile experience for deaf children. As was pointed out before, the suprasegmentals (phrasing, pitch, stress, juncture) provide invaluable clues to linguistic meaning, clues that generally escape the profoundly deaf child. In reading aloud, you are demonstrating the use of good intonation and phrasing, grouping ideas instead of reciting words. Everybody automatically uses more expression in reading aloud than in ordinary conversation. Some of the easiest and most effective ways to bring intonational patterns to the attention of deaf babies are to sing songs to them, to recite rhymes to them, and to read to them. The songs and rhymes can be very simple; they can be sensible or nonsensical, traditional or made up spontaneously. And the "storytelling" should surely be very simple. With very young children, you don't have to follow exactly the text in the book; just look at the pictures and talk about them (e.g., *Look at this great, big ball. What a nice ball. Bouncie, bouncie ballie*). The important thing is that the baby is held close and lovingly and is hearing lovely sounds in lovely patterns related to pictures in books. As the child grows older, the words themselves will also come to have meaning, particularly if the same books are read over and over again.

Attractive books on a very simple level, profuse with colorful illustrations and about themes familiar to and loved by children should be available in the schoolroom. Each week there should be several short storytelling periods. These should be informal, relaxed, and associated in the child's mind with pleasure. Children should not be *forced* to sit in on storytelling. They should be allowed to go off to another activity whenever they get restless or bored, and to stray back and rejoin the group if they wish. At the nursery level, storytelling sessions are brief and consist largely of looking at pictures and associating objects and actions with the pictures. At the kindergarten level and beyond, storytelling is a dramatic event, as exciting as going to the theater, in which words are translated into a magical sequence of characters and predicaments.

Storytelling need not take the same form every time. Frequently the teacher will read from a book. Sometimes the story may be presented through a filmstrip or movie. Sometimes the teacher may tell the story "by heart," illustrating it with drawings on paper, blackboard, or flannelboard, or using dolls and toy props to illustrate the action. Sometimes the story is told to the group as a whole, sometimes to one or a few children. The storytelling period should be enjoyable, not just a lesson in disguise. Children will become more interested if they are encouraged to participate actively in the story and "get inside" the characters and plot.

Making simple paper cutouts to use as props in telling the story can be more effective in converting words into characters and actions than merely showing the pictures in the book. The pictures choose certain highlights and are static, whereas the props can be manipulated to create sequence. If all the props for a story are put in an envelope along with the book, you will find that occasionally a child will borrow the package and retell the story alone or to a conscripted audience. We have been very successful with this technique using books such as *Mickey and Molly* by Hans Peterson, Lothrop Lee and Shepard; *My Own Little House* by Merriman B. Kaune, Follett; *What Little Anna Saw* and *When Little Anna Had a Cold* by Sandberg, Lothrop Lee and Shepard. The teacher can gradually build up a library of books and props; you will find that children delight in their use.

Hearing children return to favorite stories over and over. Many a parent has lived through having a toddler keep choosing the same book night after night for pre-bedtime reading. Both parent and child soon know the story by heart. Teachers of the deaf seem to want to keep introducing new books before the old ones have had a chance to become favorites. At Lexington some of the preschool teachers, notably Joan Godchalk and Pat Cosgrove, have developed remarkable dramatic reading sessions with their children. Stories are told to a group with great animation, and then dramatized by the children with great glee. After a few such sessions with the same story the dramatic reading becomes a real choral reading affair. The children have learned the story and tell it along with the teacher. Then a few children are selected to act it out while the rest of the class chants the story in unison. Some of the favorites have been *The Great Big Enormous Turnip* by Tolstoy, Watts; *Caps for Sale* by Slobodkin, Young Scott Books; *Play With Me* by Ets, Viking; *The Carrot Seed* by Ruth Krauss, Harper and Row; and finger plays and songs such as *Cottage in the Woods* and *Little Turtle.*

Isolating Readiness Skills

When children begin formal reading they will bring to bear the perceptual skills (visual and auditory discrimination) necessary for decoding the printed word, and the cognitive and linguistic skills necessary for comprehension at literal and inferential levels. Most of the skills needed in beginning reading should have been developed through all the normal preschool activities, especially if the teacher is aware of the component skills and is alert to use each opportunity as it presents itself to promote relevant skills.

As children play with materials and equipment, as they make things and see things on trips, as they experiment with things, they develop manual skills; they make observations as to similarities and differences of size, shape, color; they remember and relate things, exercise judgments and draw conclusions; are exposed to and use language.

However, there are some children who may need additional work to master specific skills. In such cases, it is advisable to supplement the program with specific readiness materials which provide drill for these skills. Readiness books and filmstrips, as well as teacher-made exercises, may be used. Continental Press, Inc. has some excellent materials; the reading readiness workbooks of the various basal reader series are good; the SRA's Learning to Think series is good; the Jim Handy Organization and Eye Gate House put out filmstrips with reading readiness exercises. Used selectively, such practice can be helpful.

The exercises which follow are examples of such drill.

Visual Discrimination: detecting similarities and differences

Differences may be gross or subtle; they may be of size, shape, color, direction, or internal detail (missing parts). These exercises prepare the child to detect the differences between letters and words which look essentially alike, such as p and b, was and saw.

1. Find the one that is different.

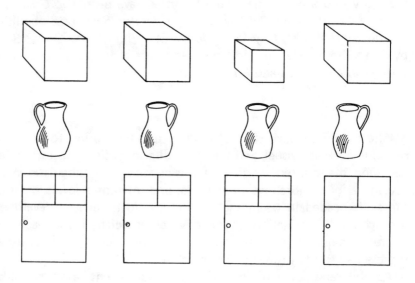

2. Find the one that is the same.

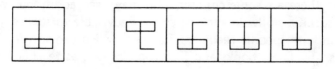

3. Draw a line between the groups that are the same.

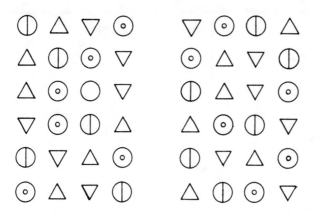

Visual motor skill, involving hand-eye coordination

1. Trace the rabbit's trail.

2. Copy the design.

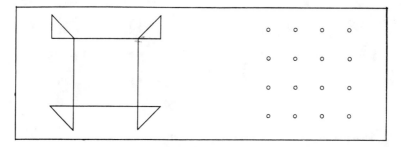

3. Complete the design.

4. Find the part that fits.

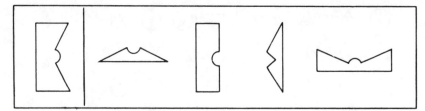

5. Continue the pattern.

Auditory Discrimination

With the deaf, especially with very young deaf children, it is questionable how much time should be spent on exercises which prepare children to discover graphemic-phonemic relations. For most deaf children, this kind of skill might better be worked on at later stages, if at all. However, there are undoubtedly some children who could benefit from auditory discrimination exercises as early as possible (during the optimal period for acquiring language through the ear). For these children, simple games might be used to call attention to initial sounds, medial vowels, rhymes, e.g.

1. Which one doesn't begin the same as the others?

2. Give the animal something that begins the same as his name.

3. Which one ends the same?

4. Which two rhyme?

Thinking Skills

The ability to organize data in various ways—to perceive relationships of cause and effect, part-whole, sequence, function—strongly affects the depth of the reading experience. Classifying and sorting things makes it much easier to remember them.

Classification

1. Make scrapbooks or picture dictionaries of foods, articles of clothing, toys, furniture, vehicles, animals.

2. Show a series of pictures, and ask the child to cross out the one that doesn't belong.

3. The child draws a line between the two that go together.

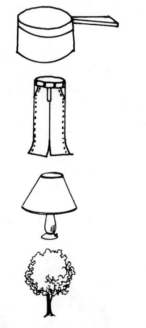

4. Show pictures of a nest, a barn, a dog house, a tepee, an igloo, a garage, a hangar. Have the child put pictures of a bird, a cow, a dog, an Indian, an Eskimo, a car, and an airplane where they belong.

5. Show a series of pictures. Have the child match the part to the whole.

6. Show a picture of a rainy day. Now show pictures of different articles of clothing. Ask the child which would be appropriate to wear when it rains.

Generalization

1. Show pictures of a farm, a zoo, a pet shop. Now show pictures of animals. Have the child put them in their appropriate places.

2. Show pictures symbolizing hot and cold. Show individual items which a child can classify as either hot or cold.

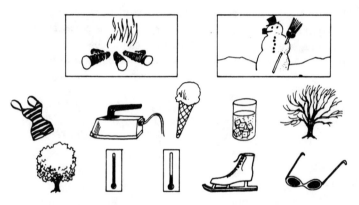

3. Draw pictures of the following objects. Have child cut and paste the right picture in the third box.

4. Cross out the one that is different.

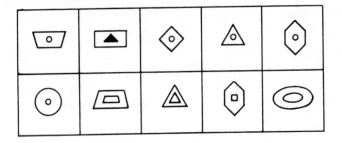

5. Make up riddles such as: A bird and an airplane are alike because they can both _____ . An apple, a ball, a clock are alike because they are all _____ . If these cannot be done verbally, use pictures. Ask the child which one doesn't belong and why.

Memory

1. The teacher may draw a simple design on the blackboard, such as

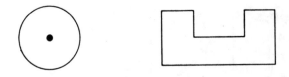

expose it for a short while, erase it, and then have the children draw it.

2. Display a series of objects in a row. Children close their eyes while you remove one object, or add one object, or switch two objects around.

3. Hide several objects around the room while children watch. Give each child a chance to find all the objects, and see who can remember where they all are.

4. Put five small blocks in a row. Tap them in an irregular sequence, as the child watches. The child then taps the blocks in the same sequence.

5. Use two identical pictures. Show one and discuss it. Now show the other picture which has had some of the items deleted. The child should identify what is missing.

6. Play concentration with cards. Cards are lined up in rows. Children take turns turning two cards face up. Whenever a child turns up a matching pair, he keeps it and gets another turn.

7. This game is played with children who have a fairly good vocabulary. The first child names a toy; the second child repeats this and names another toy, and so on, as far as the children can go. Other categories may be used.

Language

Language is best developed through constant association and use in daily activities and experiences. Some of the exercises in the reading readiness workbooks serve, however, to pinpoint specific linguistic skills such as: word, phrase, sentence recognition, subject-object differentiation, plurals, prepositions, verbs. While these language skills are not taught through these exercises, the exercises can be used diagnostically and for drill.

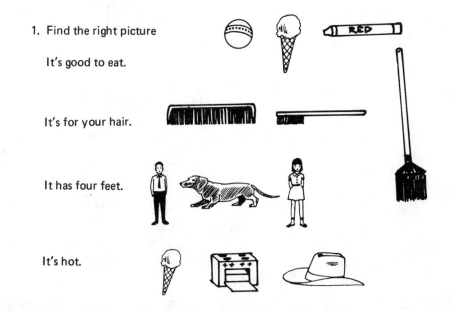

1. Find the right picture

   It's good to eat.

   It's for your hair.

   It has four feet.

   It's hot.

2. Finish the sentence.

I write with a _____.

A wagon has _____.

A _____ lives in the water.

3. Show me which picture.

The girl kisses the boy.

The ball is under the table.

The boy ran after the dog.

The boy has a book.

The girl plays with her dolls.

The girl is drinking milk.

The boy climbed the tree.

If, before children enter first grade, they have acquired some comprehension and use of language; they have been exposed to rich experiences and appropriate concepts; they have had enjoyable experiences with story books, and have observed the practical uses of the written word, they should be ready for formal instruction in reading.

DEVELOPMENTAL ACTIVITIES:

4. Primary

For deaf children, the primary years generally span the years from age 6 to 9. This is when formal reading instruction is begun. It is the level of guided reading, in which children learn to read through carefully selected, sequenced activities. Of course, the many levels of reading proficiency are developed gradually throughout the school years, or indeed, throughout life. But in the sense that printed words cease to be indistinguishable ciphers and become recognizable words with known meanings, learning to read occurs at the primary level.

The fact seems to be that most deaf children are successful in reading at the early primary level. Many parents have observed that their deaf children seem to do better in reading at 6 or 7 than their hearing children did at the same age. This is often true, but, unfortunately, it is an artifact and the gain is not sustained for long. What happens is that in order to make beginning reading possible for the 6-year-old hearing child, the language of beginning reading materials is kept quite simple, and in some cases is controlled for graphemic-phonemic equivalency. Thus, the language level is appropriate in terms of the deaf child's linguistic progress. If the sentence structure is simple and the vocabulary is concrete, the deaf child (who may be using visual decoding primarily, or even exclusively) can grasp the meaning as, or, sometimes, more easily than the hearing child (who may be using phonological as well as visual decoding). Later on, when the language in the books and stories begins to keep better pace with the hearing child's linguistic level in terms of vocabulary and sentence structure, the deaf child is overwhelmed and begins to fall way behind. This is when the problem of how to keep the deaf child's reading skills developing despite interference from the language factor rears its familiar, ugly head. But for a while, at the primary level, teaching reading can be terribly gratifying because both teacher and pupil can experience success. How to continue on this course is the very special problem of the teacher of the deaf.

Aims

The general aim is to maintain children's motivation and interest in books at a high level, and to systematically improve their ability to read by helping them master specific reading skills and techniques. This means the language and reading programs must be intimately and intricately interrelated. The language program will provide sequenced experiences to promote conceptual and linguistic growth. The reading program will provide developmental and remedial activities to build reading skills that children can apply in recreational and functional reading. These skills involve:
1. acquiring a constantly growing sight vocabulary
2. using various word recognition techniques
3. developing the habit of reading ideas in thought units
4. visualizing what is read
5. developing an ability to read and understand longer units

Making the Transition From Informal to Formal Reading

Formal reading (that is, holding children responsible for decoding written language) is not introduced at the very outset. However, from the very outset, children are bombarded with the written word. As the program of activities and games begun in the preschool continues in the primary school, the primary teacher, unlike the preschool teacher, begins to accompany these activities with writing along with the normal conversation that goes on. The words and sentences used in language activities (e.g., "news"), social studies activities (e.g., projects about family, food, holidays, etc.), science activities (e.g., experiments with plants, shadows, electricity, etc.), are written on the board, on oaktag and newsprint, on cards, and in teacher-made books. Because the written language bears a one-to-one relationship with the spoken language and all the word meanings are known to the children, little by little many of these words become sight words; that is, the children recognize and identify the meanings of the written words at sight. When the same words appear and reappear (by chance, or by teacher contrivance, as when the teacher has examined the vocabulary of the stories that the children will soon be asked to read and has carefully implanted these words into the ongoing activities) they soon become old friends, recognized without agonizing scrutiny. In addition, when children are reading the functional materials produced in these activities but stumble over some of the words, the teacher helps them figure out what these words say by encouraging them to use context clues, configurational clues, key features, known parts within the word, and, with some children, phonics clues.

The vocabulary of oral and written words that emerges from all these sources should be quite extensive, ranging from the concrete to the abstract and including every part of speech to identify the objects, people, actions, feelings, and observations involved in the various experiences. To keep track of all these words, the teacher should set up some temporary recording system—hanging a sheet of newsprint on a certain wall or reserving a particular section of blackboard on which to quickly jot down the words that come up—and some permanent recording system such as taking time once a week to enter these words into booklets or on cards arranged by categories (toys, foods, feelings, outdoors words, accident words, holiday words, etc.). Pictures should, of course, accompany the words. These vocabulary books and boxes can serve as reference sources, much like dictionaries, for the children. They can also be used in games to reinforce word meaning and sight vocabulary. The teacher can send the words home to the parents periodically and enlist the parents as allies in promoting vocabulary by making scrapbooks and playing word games.

It will not take very long before most children in the class have acquired a respectable sight vocabulary of common words and have adopted the habit of reading familiar language when it is written. The teacher can then supplement all these teacher-made and functional reading materials with more formal materials, such as basal readers, library books, worksheets, children's newspapers, filmstrips.

Meanwhile, of course, the storytelling sessions have been going ahead full steam. The selections can be longer, the stories more intricate, but the major goal still is to intrigue and spellbind children with the treasures available to them through books. Dramatization can become more formalized, with the children putting on shows and using printed programs to identify the cast and scenes. Also, the teacher may sometimes choose a longer story and read it serially instead of in one sitting.

The Language Arts Program

A brief outline of the language arts program should give some idea of the enormous possibilities for promoting conceptual and linguistic growth, as well as specifically indicating how reading can be tied in with the daily activities.

"News" Reporting

The news period should be regarded as a conversation period, in which personal and impersonal items are shared and chatted about in much the same way that adults communicate with each other in socializing. As children generally enjoy telling about their new possessions and about where they went and what they did with their families and friends, the news period affords an excellent opportunity for meaningful repetition of simple language patterns in oral and written form.

Although it is not necessary to do so, we have found it helpful to separate news reporting into two separate activities, one for group news and one for individual news. This may have the effect of reducing the conversational exchange among the children, but it has two advantages. For one thing, it reduces the amount of time that children must sit together in a group, thus imposing more realistic demands on their attention span; and for another, it represents the group news sheet as something resembling a newspaper. (In fact, this activity can be developed into a class newspaper at the intermediate level, and a school newspaper at the advanced level.)

The group news sheet, a piece of newsprint tacked up on the blackboard, generally begins with some calendar work to identify the day of the week and the date. Other standard items that get recorded are those relating to the weather, the attendance, and any regular or special activities the class will engage in that day. Any other items, including personal or individual ones, that the children want to contribute to the news sheet should also be recorded. At the beginning, the teacher will probably have to answer as well as ask the questions that elicit the items to be written. But as the children become familiar with the procedure and with the language for the repetitive events, they will dictate the sentences for the teacher to write. Seeing your words get written one by one is an enormous impetus to reading. At first, the sentences are very simple, stating the bare facts. But gradually variations in language and content can be introduced, always keeping pace with the children's progress. An example of an early and a later news sheet may show the potential of this medium.

Today is Thursday, September 23. It's a sunny day. Eddie is not in school today. We go to Art today.

Today is Thursday, February 4.
  It's sunny, but cold.
  Everybody is here today, except Eddie. He has a sore throat.
  We go to Art right after lunch today. Maybe we will make collages.
  Rita's mother is visiting school today. We are happy she is here.

The group news sheet lends itself to the introduction of new vocabulary items and new sentence constructions because the natural recurrence of items provides the repetition needed to fix the forms in the children's linguistic repertoire. Then the teacher can present new ways of saying the same thing using new vocabulary and transforming kernel sentences through negation, phrases and clauses (e.g., Eddie is not here. Eddie is absent. Eddie is still absent. Eddie didn't come to school all week because he has a sore throat.).

The group news sheet also promotes reading. At first the children "read" it from memory using whatever picture clues are available. Gradually, as the words are repeated, they become part of the children's sight vocabulary. The teacher also uses every opportunity to show children how to use contextual clues and other word recognition skills to figure out words they don't recognize at sight. The teacher may also quiz the children on specific words and phrases. This builds an understanding of question forms and an ability to pick out specific answers to questions. (e.g., How many children are not here today? Which word tells who didn't come to school? Where does it tell why? Where will we go today? Which words tell when? Why is Rita's mother here?) The children soon learn when a one-word answer is enough and when a phrase or sentence is called for.

For individual news, each child has a "Tell Mommy" book (really a "Tell Mommy and Daddy; Tell Teacher" book). This traditional lined composition book goes back and forth between school and home each day. Some time during the day the teacher sits down with each child and elicits something to tell Mommy and Daddy. At the very beginning both the idea and the language will have to be suggested by the teacher (e.g., Shall we tell Mommy and Daddy what we made today?) with the teacher recording any response the child contributes (We made oatmeal cookies today. I didn't like them.). The child "reads" the item with teacher's help, and illustrates it. At home, the child shows and "reads" it to the parents. They, in turn, follow the same procedure and write up something the child did at home to tell the teacher. Pretty soon the ideas will come from the child, with the teacher and parents providing the written language. Gradually, the child will be able to dictate both the ideas and the language, and will be able to read the entry with just a little help. Sometimes the teacher may sit with two children at a time to read together what Mommy and Daddy wrote and to compose new items for Mommy and Daddy. Then conversations that go beyond the simple recorded items can take place.

Direct Experiences

As children mature, their concepts of time, distance, causal, logical, and interpersonal relations develop. The outline which follows gives a slight indication of the kinds of vocabulary and concepts that can emerge through planned direct experiences.

1. Trips

   a) Stores (pet, grocery, bakery, five and ten, department, drug, barber shop, beauty parlor, florist, delicatessen, cafeteria, shoe, restaurant, tailor, hardware, etc.)

   Vocabulary—to come, to go, to see, to buy, to sell, to pay, there is, there are, there was, there were, to want, to have, clerk, package, money, cash register, counter, shelf, pretty, delicious, etc.

   Concepts—a little, a lot, many, few, some, too much, not enough, expensive, heavy, light.

b) Zoo

Vocabulary—Names of animals. Habitat: cage, tree, ocean, cave. Food for animals. Actions: jump, swim, climb, fly. Parts of body: head, tail, trunk, beak, claws, feathers, fur. Sounds: roar, bark, growl. Size and color: striped, spotted, etc.

Concepts—Wild, tame. Natural habitat of animals. Climate. Geography on simple level.

c) Farm

Vocabulary—Names of animals. Names of farm buildings and machinery: barn, coop, tractor. Vegetables, fruits, etc.

Concepts—Mother and baby. How food is produced. Products derived from planting. Products derived from animals.

d) Community helpers

(1) Police station

Vocabulary—Policeman, cop, uniform, police car, siren, traffic, ticket, fine, etc.

Concepts—Obeying rules, punishments, protection.

(2) Fire station

Vocabulary—Fireman, uniform, fire engine, siren, hose, pump, smoke, burn, alarm, drill, etc.

Concepts—How fires start, how they are put out.

(3) Post Office

Vocabulary—Letter, post card, envelope, stamp, address, mailbox, airmail, postmark, etc.

Concepts—Time, distance, how a letter travels, fast, faster, far, near, local, rural, foreign.

e) Transportation

Vocabulary—Bus, subway, train, taxi, ferry, airplane, ticket, transfer, driver, ride, road, ocean, river, lake, etc.

Concepts—What makes things go, speed, distance.

f) Other trips

Park, playground, parade, museums, hospital, theater, movie, TV studio, dock, factory, walks to see a bridge, tunnel, construction project.

2. Activities

a) Science

Caring for pets, planting seeds, collecting leaves and rocks, learning about insects, weather, seasons, color-prism, rainbow, shadows, experiments with water, magnets, air.

b) Health

Foods—Classification (fruits, vegetables, dairy products, meat, etc.) Foods appropriate for each meal. Simple nutrition. Eating manners. Care of teeth, hair, nails. Proper clothing. Cleanliness.

c) Safety

In school—walking in line, keeping to right, looking ahead. Outdoors—traffic rules. On playground. At home—matches, scissors, hammer and nails.

d) Holidays

Birthdays, Thanksgiving, Easter, Christmas. Patriotic holidays. Simple history.

e) People

Where people live. Simple street maps. Finding different states on map. Finding other countries. Studying about American Indians and people of other lands.

3. Projects

> Building things, making a snowman, flying a kite, making collections, making scrapbooks, developing hobbies, putting on a party, putting on a show or exhibit, making Christmas decorations, cooking puddings, making applesauce, cocoa, popcorn, cheese, making presents out of paper, cardboard, wool, clay, scraps of material, wire, pipe cleaners.

In the planning, execution and follow-up of these trips and activities, reading and writing may be brought in, in many different ways:

1. Books and stories about similar experiences can be read.

2. Letters may be written in conjunction with some of the activities: to request permission or information; invitations; thank-you letters; letters telling an absent child or a former teacher about the trip.

3. Lists can be made on the blackboard or on newsprint or oak tag: lists of questions; lists of things to look for on the trip; lists of materials needed; duty lists; lists of the steps and procedures in carrying out projects and plans.

4. Bulletin board items: posters related to activities; samples of children's work; announcements of events; letters received; newspaper and magazine items of interest in connection with trips, activities, and projects; graphs and charts of weather, height, or weight, menus.

5. Signs, labels, and captions: At this level, the child is not merely exposed to printed symbols but is expected to take active note of them wherever they occur. The printed symbols give added meaning to the activity, and the activity in turn supplies meanings for the symbols. For example, in a trip to the supermarket to get the ingredients for a cooking project, the children can try to find the items on a What We Need list by looking at the signs hanging overhead in each aisle.

6. Experience stories may be made by the teacher with the children to record the experiences of the trip. Although the teacher should attempt to elicit from the children a sequential account of the experience, they should be allowed every freedom in giving their own impressions. Sometimes what seems to the teacher to be the most important element in the trip is not what has registered uppermost in the minds of the youngsters. A parent who lived near our school

invited our class to lunch one day. We had a lovely time. When we returned to school and discussed our experience preparatory to writing a thank-you note and a picture story about our trip, I discovered that what had impressed the children most was the swift elevator with the heart-sinking drops. This became the featured element in our story.

The experience chart should be the expression of the children's impressions, discoveries, and reactions. The teacher should act as recorder, and coordinate the impressions of all the children. In this way the experience chart becomes a unique description of this particular event with these particular children, rather than a generalized version of any trip. When the story records what has been most significant to the children they will more easily read the printed symbols. These books and charts may be illustrated in a variety of ways—by children's drawings, by actual photographs, by pictures cut out of magazines.

The following experience story was made by a Lower School class after their trip to the pet shop:

THE PET SHOP
We went to the pet shop   Tuesday morning.

We walked in two straight lines.

In the store we saw many dogs   ,

cats   , birds   , and fish

We bought two 2 turtles   for our school-

room   . We named one SLOW   and the other

POKE   . We will feed them.

They will grow bigger.

7. Teacher-made books growing out of trips, activities, experiments, projects. For example: What's Round and What's Square?; What's Red and What's Green?; What Has Wheels?; How Does It Feel?; Our Lucky Day; etc. These books should be made with the children, and should, as much as possible, record the children's own language and observations. The teacher asks questions to focus and organize the experience and records each child's response, usually on a separate page so the child can illustrate the written sentence. The book can then be bound together and a title page made. We include these books in the class library, pasting a library lending card in the back. The children enjoy taking them home to read to their parents. One book which had a long list of borrowers was named "The Candy Apples That Tasted Awful." It recorded what happened when the class made candy apples but left the syrup mix boiling in the pot until it burned. The project was repeated a second time, this time successfully, and a second book was made, entitled "The Candy Apples That Tasted Good." This book was not nearly as popular as the first one.

Another teacher-made book which became a great favorite emerged from an accidental occurrence which the teacher was alert enough to capitalize on. A child had come to school with a brand new attaché case which she was enormously proud of. She was especially delighted that it had a key with which she could lock it. All day that attaché case accompanied the child during all her activities. When the class went to Rhythms, the attaché case went right along. The Rhythms teacher duly admired it, and then told the child to put it aside. But the child would not be parted from the key, and all during the dances the tightly clutched key impeded her movements. Finally the teacher took the key from the child. To reassure her that this was only a temporary separation, she placed it in plain sight on the top of the piano. The inevitable happened. During a particularly lively crescendo the key dropped into the piano! No one's hand was thin enough to reach through the piano keys to retrieve the key. The child was crushed, her classmates stunned, the teacher mortified. Finally, one of the children thought of a solution. She knew another child who had the same attaché case. She was immediately dispatched to borrow that key. Everyone waited with bated breath. When she came back, they tried the key, and it worked! The teacher promised she would borrow the key from its owner and get a new one made to replace the lost key.

When the class got back to their own room after Rhythms, this marvelous story tumbled out. The teacher wrote it up and all the children illustrated it. A library borrowing slip pasted into the back cover made it a circulating book. Later, the teacher was able to extend the children's enthusiasm by reading to them E. B. White's *Stuart Little*, a story about someone who might have been able to crawl into the piano and retrieve the lost key. Of course, these children learned a second meaning for the word key, and their favorite riddle for a while became What has keys but no locks?

The Formal Program

Functional reading and teacher-made materials emerging from class activities of all kinds are the backbone of the reading program for the deaf child because they offer the opportunity to learn (or teach) sequential reading skills using known language. This is true not only at beginning reading levels but all through the elementary school years. Hopefully, the reading skills acquired in this way are applied to normal reading matter to the degree that is possible within the limits imposed by linguistic stumbling blocks. The children need to be given every opportunity to read appropriate materials of all kinds, ranging from comic books to workbooks, readers, and library books. Since this is the level of guided reading, the teacher will carefully nurse their reading skills along, making whatever provision needs to be made for language difficulties. In other words, the child is encouraged to read constantly, using the best skills possible; the teacher has to determine whether a difficulty that arises is due to a reading deficiency or whether it is due to a linguistic deficiency.

The primary child cannot be expected to cope with unknown language while reading. The teacher may use reading as a source of language stimulation, either by integrating the anticipated new vocabulary and constructions into language and other class activities beforehand, or by explaining them as they come up during the reading and then entering them in the various recording systems the class has been using for new language. Since most deaf children will almost inevitably have some difficulty with normal commercial materials, it may be hard for the teacher to get a clear and precise picture of how much the child is comprehending and what reading skills the child is using. It takes practice and skill and long and close observation of children for the teacher to become accomplished in this task. Until this happens, reading sessions may be arduous and unrewarding for both teacher and child. The only thing to do in such a case is to keep the session short, breaking up the reading into several sittings, and introduce other types of reading (e.g., storytelling) to restore reading in good favor. Perhaps teachers will be less discouraged if they can keep in mind that the easiest (if not only) way to promote reading skills is with material in which the language is known; when reading is used to promote language growth, it is difficult to promote reading at the same time. Setting realistic goals can help.

When the formal reading program is begun, there is generally a specific period set aside for the children to engage in reading. This period may involve a group lesson, with all the children participating; it may be a group lesson in which half of the group participates while the other children do other things (which may or may not be reading); or it may be a period during which the teacher reads with just one child at a time while the other children do other things (including reading). Whichever way it is conducted, the teacher has selected and prepared some particular reading matter to present. It may be the same material for all the children (e.g., an item in *My Weekly Reader,* or a poem from the basal reader, or directions for making something, etc.), or it may be different for each child. The teacher will be guided by the interests and needs of the children.

Whatever material has been chosen, the first thing the teacher should do is to give the children a chance to read the material on their own. Very often the teacher interprets the material for the children before they have had a chance to really examine it. As the children read to themselves (or aloud) the teacher observes them, making mental or written note of their habits, strengths, and weaknesses. Then the teacher makes some attempt to assess their level of comprehension (through discussion, oral or written questions, dramatization). At this point, after it has become clear to the teacher what the children have been able to do on their own, they may be filled in on whatever they may have missed (in terms of language if it was not pretaught, or in terms of concepts or inferences). A record should be kept for each child on what was read and on progress made.

The general procedure to be followed in a reading lesson will vary from time to time, from child to child, and especially from one kind of material to another. On any one day, the teacher may decide to use a story in a basal reader; or do individual reading in library books; or use *My Weekly Reader*; or a workbook or teacher-made exercise; a filmstrip; a story from a book or magazine; or an experience chart. The variations are innumerable, but whatever is used, the teacher should clearly know which skills are being promoted and where each child stands in relation to these skills.

Basal Readers

The use of a basal reader series, as well as supplementary readers from other series, can be very profitable in a well-balanced reading program. Many of these books have been prepared by well-known children's authors, under the supervision of reading experts. Such readers present a wide variety of reading activities organized sequentially and developmentally to provide for continuity in growth in reading skills, habits, and attitudes. Although they may be difficult for the deaf child, the vocabulary and sentence structure are controlled to allow for gradual increase in difficulty.

The content is generally based on children's interests; but a standard text cannot meet the interests of every child in the class, nor even the interests of the class as a whole in the same way that other materials can. Although they have improved considerably recently, readers are generally not as attractive as library books. Therefore, basal readers should be supplemented by library books and functional materials to provide a stimulating reading program.

Manuals accompanying the basic readers are excellent guides. They provide suggestions for the development of the stories, as well as ideas for supplementary activities. Although these manuals are more helpful to the teacher of the hearing child, the teacher of the deaf child should be able to adapt such ideas as may be useful.

Despite the fact that the stories progress from easy to hard, the teacher may want to skip around in the basal reader using selected stories. There are language pitfalls for the deaf student in most of these stories, and sometimes it is better to start with a story that has intrinsic interest rather than with one that may be somewhat easier.

Depending on content and reading challenge, the way in which the reading is conducted should vary. At times, the story should be read as a whole without interruption for pure enjoyment of its general content; the checking on comprehension should be brief, and might be conducted through dramatization. Sometimes the story should be read in sections, with questions at the stopping points to aid comprehension and clarify the story thread. Sometimes the story is read line by line, with each idea interpreted.

Sometimes very little checking on comprehension and specific reading skills will be undertaken, and at other times a great deal of testing may be done. There is no hard and fast rule. The teacher should read a story and determine the best treatment. In general, a gentle balance has to be worked out between using a story for progress in reading skills and using a story for reading enjoyment. If both can be accomplished together, so much the better. If, however, a choice must be made, it is usually wiser to give enough help so that the story is enjoyed, and leave the developing of skills for another device (e.g., teacher-made exercises). If those words and expressions which may cause trouble are taught in advance of the reading, the child is more likely to have a successful reading experience. The teacher should remember that lessons in a basal reader constitute only one facet of the reading program. What cannot be accomplished through this activity, may be achieved in another way.

With the caution that flexibility is most important, a general outline of procedures in using a basal reader is presented. The teacher is encouraged—even urged—to depart from this method at any time.

1. Preparing for Reading

a) The teacher should see to it that the child has had the experiential background to understand the facts and concepts of the story.

b) The teacher must be sure that the words, idiomatic expressions and peculiarities of sentence structure (e.g., *Over the fence went the pig.*) do not render the story almost meaningless to the deaf child.

If the teacher has chosen the story because of its intrinsic interest and appropriateness for the child, there are various options for coping with linguistic difficulties. If the language problems are overwhelming, the teacher should not burden the child with them but should use the story for recreational reading in a storytelling session. If the language difficulties are serious but not overwhelming, and the new words and expressions are not just "storybook words" but would be generally useful in the child's language repertoire, an effort should be made to preteach this language in advance. Through meaningful activities the children can gain a working familiarity with the language when they get to it. If the language problems are minimal, they can be ignored and the teacher can provide the child with the unknown meanings during the actual reading.

c) Finally, it is a good idea to stimulate an interest and provide motivation for the reading before the reading takes place. Oral discussion, a trip, a film, pictures, related books, or a project may serve to provide the experiential background to prepare the child for the language and content of the story, and to link the story to the child's life in some way. Before reading a story about *The Magic Word* (please), one teacher brought in some magic tricks for the children to play with (a penny that could be made to disappear by "abracadabra").

2. Guided Reading

a) The child should have an opportunity to read uninterruptedly in order to follow the sequence and get a general idea of the story.

b) Then the teacher and the child may go back over the story and discuss it. This will indicate whether the child caught the main idea, and will reveal areas of difficulty. The teacher can then tackle the difficulties. This may mean going back to reread specific parts of the story with the teacher helping the child to interpret unknown language and to use known reading skills.

3. Follow-up

To reinforce memory for the ideas and language of the story, any of these approaches may be used:

a) Dramatization—informally by teacher and child, or more formally as a rehearsed dramatic presentation.

b) Having the child draw pictures to illustrate the story—casually, or more formally—pasted in a book or on a roll of paper for retelling to the group.

c) Workbooks accompanying the basal reader provide follow-up exercises for vocabulary and reading skills.

d) Teacher-made exercises of all kinds, using the vocabulary and checking on literal and inferential comprehension.

e) Interests may be extended through other activities. The story may stimulate an interest in other stories or poems related to the subject. Scrapbooks or projects may be initiated based on an idea in the story (e.g., constructing circus figures out of pipe cleaners).

The following exercises illustrate one procedure in using a basal reader story, "The Missing Necklace," Level 3, Book A, illustrated by Phoebe Moore, Glenview, Ill., Scott, Foresman and Co., 1971.

The story tells about a picnic lunch to which Mrs. Pig has invited her friends—three turtles, a chipmunk, a sheep and a cat. When lunch is over, someone discovers that Mrs. Pig's necklace, made of marshmallows, is missing. The chipmunk acts as detective and interrogates everyone. They discover that Mrs. Pig has eaten her own necklace.

In this case, the children first would read the story on their own, without any teacher help. They would then answer the written questions, giving the teacher some idea of their general grasp of the story. A guided reading session would follow, with teacher and children reading and interpreting the story together through discussion and dramatization. The children would then answer a second battery of questions that test comprehension and memory of the details and ideas of the story.

I. Worksheet to be completed by the children after independent reading:

    A.   Draw these pictures:

a turtle	a chipmunk
a sheep	marshmallows
a sandwich	a thermos
a necklace	purple

    B.   Write which sentence is 1st, 2nd, 3rd, 4th, 5th.

    Then draw a picture for each sentence.

    Mrs. Pig wore a marshmallow necklace. ☐

    Three turtles, a chipmunk, a sheep and
a cat came to Mrs. Pig's house. ☐

    Mrs. Pig's necklace was missing. ☐

    Mrs. Pig invited her friends to lunch. ☐

    Mrs. Pig made sandwiches and Kool-Aid. ☐

    C.   Finish the sentences.

    Mrs. Pig's necklace was made of _____.

        sandwiches
        marshmallows
        detective

The necklace was missing because _____.

> Mrs. Pig ate it
> The chipmunk took it
> Mrs. Pig lost it

This is a _____ story.

> sad
> true
> funny

II. Worksheet to be completed by the children after guided reading:

1. Mrs. Pig invited her friends for _____.

   > Thanksgiving dinner
   > lunch
   > a birthday party

2. _____ friends came to Mrs. Pig's house.

   > 6, 7, 3

3. The lunch was _____.

   > in the house
   > outside
   > at school

4. For lunch, Mrs. Pig made _____.

   > marshmallows
   > sandwiches
   > detective

5. They drank _____.

   > orange juice
   > soda
   > Kool-Aid

6. The Kool-Aid was cold because _____.

        it had ice
        it was in the refrigerator
        it was in the thermos

7. Mrs. Pig made a necklace of _____.

        sandwiches
        marshmallows
        detective

8. The necklace was missing because it was _____.

        eaten
        lost
        beautiful

Even harder version: The necklace was missing because

        _____ _____ it.
            1   2

        1. Mrs. Pig   the chipmunk   the cat
        2. lost   wore   ate

9. The cat ate _____.

  The turtles ate _____.

  Mrs. Pig ate _____.

        sandwiches
        marshmallows
        a peach
        a radish

10. Mrs. Pig was _____.

        funny   sad   tired

11. Name 4 foods at the lunch:

      1.   3.
      2.   4.

12. Name 4 animals at the lunch:

      1.   3.
      2.   4.

13. Draw Mrs. Pig just before   Draw Mrs. Pig when the
    the lunch.   lunch was over.

Workbooks

Commercially prepared workbooks (independent of the basal reader) can have a place in the reading program if the teacher is aware of their limitations and uses them judiciously. These workbooks provide simple, ready-to-use assignments. They present opportunities for drill in specific vocabularies. Children frequently enjoy the "grown-up" feeling they get from using workbook materials independently.

If the teacher trains children in the use of workbooks, they may develop good habits of working independently and neatly. Children should be permitted to progress at their own rate. The teacher should carefully examine the different types of workbooks and choose those that seem to best suit the children's needs for vocabulary development and drill in specific skills. However, as with any non-teacher-made materials, a workbook does not always meet individual needs. It is not necessary to proceed through a workbook consecutively. The teacher may want to omit some pages or vary the order of using the pages. The teacher may find that cutting out specific pages will provide drill for those children who need additional practice in some areas. Also, some of the pages which can't be used as they appear in the workbook may be adapted.

Periodicals

Periodical materials, such as *Surprise, My Weekly Reader No. 1, News Pilot,* and *News Ranger* can be very useful at this level. They acquaint the child with the function of a newspaper. Children become accustomed to receiving the publication regularly, and begin the newspaper-reading habit. The interest level of the material is generally high. The publications offer a wide variety of topics and present opportunities for developing concepts in current events, health, science, and social studies on a simple but meaningful level.

The teacher can also use this material for developing specific skills in reading. For example:

1. Reading for different purposes: to enjoy the humor, to get the main idea, to answer specific questions, etc.

2. Picture interpretation: some of the comic strips and other items are particularly well adapted to developing a sense of humor, making associations, reasoning, forming judgments and attitudes.

3. Finding or underlining words, phrases, or sentences that tell where, why, when, etc.

4. Identifying new words using word recognition skills, content clues and picture clues.

Audio-Visual Materials

An enormous quantity and variety of audio-visual aids are currently available and can be advantageously used in the reading program. For a generation of children brought up on TV, audio-visual materials are highly motivational. Selected and used wisely, they can be an excellent source of information and learning. Transparencies, slides, films, and filmstrips are produced in abundance at every level on every subject for every purpose. Many filmstrip companies have produced series that are designed to provide drill in specific reading skills. Also, many attractive classic and modern stories are available on filmstrips. Of course, the captioned film program for the deaf is very useful, and the teacher can capitalize on the high interest generated by these films to introduce the books on which the films are based. These materials can be used independently by children, with or without follow-up activities provided by the teacher; it depends on whether the material is used recreationally to stimulate interests, or developmentally to stimulate concepts and skills. Or, the materials can be used by the teacher with one or more children in guided lessons.

From my point of view, one of the most valuable contributions to the reading program are the book-record-filmstrip combinations put out by some companies. Reading a story, listening to it, and seeing it can be very exciting reading experiences, contributing both to motivation and comprehension. At the Lexington School, many teachers have tape recorders on which they themselves have recorded the text of selected stories. Children take a book and turn on the recorder and listen to their own teacher "tell" the story.

Another approach that has been used very successfully to enhance the language-reading program is having children create their own animated filmstrips. They can write their own stories, or adapt stories they have read, and create the props using clay or pipe cleaners and other materials. There is nothing as exciting as producing a movie of your own and proudly showing and interpreting it to your friends and neighbors. Some of our poorest readers have been inspired to outdo themselves using this technique. The librarian, or A-V specialist, if there is one in the school, can be of enormous help in acquainting teachers with this rich source of materials and in helping them to use these aids in many ways.

Library Books

The ultimate test of the success of any reading program is whether the child voluntarily becomes a regular library subscriber. It is not enough to teach children *how* to read, as hard as that may be; it is important to addict them to the habit of reading. Reading lessons and reading drills alone cannot do this. Exposure to the rich array of beautiful books available to them on library shelves can excite the children's curiosity and interest and can demonstrate that reading can satisfy a wide range of interests, needs, and abilities. Trips to the neighborhood library can initiate this very important habit and way of life. A well-stocked school library and a knowledgeable librarian can contribute heavily to the success of the reading program.

At the Lexington School, in addition to child- or teacher-initiated visits that may be casual, voluntary, deliberate or purposeful, each primary class is invited to spend one period a week in the school library. This gives children a chance to become familiar with the facilities and uses of the library and to avail themselves of library materials. They are given time to look through the books and to choose books to take out for the week. The librarian may select books that will be of special interest to the particular class and display them on a table. The children also have access to the open shelves, of course. During the library period at the primary level, the librarian reads the children a story or shows them a film. Then they may dramatize it together. It is very easy to judge the success of this activity by how many children clamor to be allowed to take the book home.

In addition to the library books that the children are permitted to take home, the teacher usually has a stock of library books in the reading corner of the classroom. The teacher selects books which are both simple and interesting and which relate to individual children's interests or to class activities. The books are changed periodically to keep enthusiasm high and to keep pace with new interests. These books may be used in many different ways and for both recreational and developmental reading purposes. Children may browse in the reading corner during free choice time and choose a library book to look through. Sometimes, the child may simply pick up the book, look through the pictures, and put the book back. Sometimes the child may read it right through, with or without asking the teacher for help. Sometimes the teacher does a follow-up on such voluntary reading. Sometimes the follow-up consists of a short discussion to elicit the child's reaction to the book and record the name of the book on a Book Worm chart. Sometimes the teacher may put a few key questions inside the book for the child to answer on a voluntary or required basis.

In another use of library books, the teacher may select a specific book to read with a specific child during individual reading. In this case, the child usually reads the book aloud to the teacher, and discussions follow each reading session. The book may be completed in one or more sessions, and the child may use a self-made bookmark to mark where reading stopped. At the beginning of the next individual session, the teacher may help the child review the plot and vocabulary before continuing with the reading. Unless the book turns out to be too difficult or takes too long to complete, children usually get a lot of satisfaction from this type of reading and enjoy adding new titles to their list of read books.

The teacher may also use the books from the reading corner for pure recreational reading in storytelling sessions. This enables the teacher to choose a book that the children would enjoy (maybe one they saw on TV or in the movies) but cannot read on their own. The story may be told in one session, or it may be serialized. If the teacher is dramatic enough and the book appropriate enough, interest can be sustained over a relatively long period. During the telling, children should be encouraged to visualize the characters and the action, to follow and remember the sequence, to predict outcomes. In time, they will develop skill in retelling the story orally, through dramatization, or through drawings.

Dramatization following (and sometimes during) the telling of the story is an invaluable device. It gives children an opportunity to project into the story, to imagine the emotions and personalities of the characters, and to reproduce their conversation. In acting out the story, children remember the chief idea, the mood, and the important details and incidents in their proper sequence.

Library books should also be used with social studies and science activities. With these, the teacher must help to interpret the text, but this use of library books gives the primary child an excellent beginning in the use of reference materials and in reading for information.

Teacher-made Exercises Isolating Reading Skills

In developing reading skills through the use of all the usual reading materials, the deaf child is sometimes faced with too many complexities all at once. Unknown vocabulary and language forms often interfere with the step-by-step mastery of reading skills. It is therefore advisable for the teacher to provide easier materials for the sequential development of skills. By constructing special exercises, the teacher can usually eliminate complicating factors and focus on one process at a time. After isolating skills for remediation, the teacher should watch to see whether there is a carry-over from such exercises to normal reading matter. Examples of activities to promote the various skills follow. Keep in mind that the primary level covers a span of three years, and that these exercises were designed for use during the various stages within this span.

Sight Vocabulary

The term "sight vocabulary" refers to the total number of printed words that the child can identify at sight. The child's ability to read in thought units will depend on how quickly and easily words are recognized. If the child has to stop to figure out every third or fourth word, it interferes with grasping the meaning of the whole sentence.

The particular words in a sight reading vocabulary vary from child to child. However, children should be familiar with the words they will encounter in early reading materials. Every child's sight vocabulary should increase steadily and constantly.

How do children acquire a sight vocabulary? They may be given drill through flash cards and workbook exercises. Or they may accumulate a sight reading vocabulary by seeing certain words repeated many times in meaningful settings in all the normal classroom activities. If the teacher maintains a system for storing all the vocabulary that comes up in conversation, news work, science and social studies activities, and reading, this not only reinforces the children's memory for those words, but provides a way of keeping tabs on the children's growing vocabularies. Very frequently, the words which a child learns to recognize on sight are those that are richest in associations and not necessarily those which are most frequently repeated. For example, the hardest words to differentiate are words which actually recur constantly—short monosyllables such as prepositions and articles (in, or, at, an, it, these, etc.) and words lacking concrete referents (just, but, or). These words depend on contextual and syntactic clues and develop with growing linguistic sophistication rather than with drill. However, vocabulary games and exercises can be fun in themselves, and they can help sustain an interest in and memory for words. Some examples follow:

1. Lotto—Children are given cards with words printed on them. Each child's card is different, but many of the words recur on the various cards. The teacher has a box of pictures to go with the words. The teacher, or a child, picks pictures from the box at random, showing them to the players. Whoever has the word for the picture covers that square with a blank tab. The first child to cover the entire card wins.

doll	shoe	girl	coat
baby	boy	house	comb
horse	cat	sun	apple

2. Concentration—The teacher makes a set of about 16 cards, printing the word on one card and pasting the matching picture on another card. The players shuffle the cards and place them in rows

face down on a table. Players take turns turning up two cards. If they are a pair, the player keeps them. If not, they are turned face down again. When all the matching pairs have been chosen, the player with the most cards wins.

3. The teacher makes up cards with pictures. In a separate envelope, the teacher puts the matching words for all the cards. A child chooses a card and then looks through the envelope for the appropriate words. The words are placed on the pictures. The teacher may check the child's work, or the children may use the vocabulary books or cards, or a picture dictionary, to check their own work.

4. Each page has a picture and a slot into which the child inserts the word. Pages may be kept in alphabetical order. Words may be stored in an envelope pasted on the inside front cover.

airplane

5. Color the balloons.

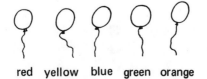

red   yellow   blue   green   orange

6. Draw a circle around the right picture.

table	![daisies]	![table]	![window]	![clock]
flowers	![table]	![house]	![tree]	![flowers]
chair	![chair]	![table]	![house]	![window]
window	![clock]	![door]	![window]	![flowers]
clock	![book]	![clock]	![chair]	![bed]

7. Draw a line from the word to the picture.

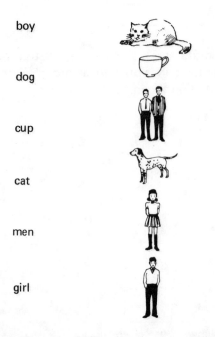

boy

dog

cup

cat

men

girl

8. Rummy—The teacher makes a set of about 50 cards by writing the names of ten different items in five categories on each card (e.g., foods, colors, animals, clothes, parts of the body). To play the game, the children deal out five cards to each player (from two to five players can play together), putting the rest of the deck face down in the middle. They then take turns picking the top card off the deck. If they want it, they keep it and discard another card from their hand by putting it face up beside the deck. If they don't want the card they drew, they just put it face up beside the deck. The first child to get five cards in any one category wins.

9. Cross out the word that doesn't belong:

a. bus	car	book	truck	airplane
b. wood	hot	warm	cool	cold
c. apple	orange	banana	pea	peach
d. father	face	aunt	sister	brother
e. girl	boy	man	woman	tree
f. comb	hair	thumb	ear	nose
g. lion	lamb	tiger	elephant	giraffe

10. Draw a line between the two words that go together.

brush	socks
bread	read
shoes	comb
hat	stars
moon	socks
book	hands
gloves	butter

11. Draw a line between the two words that are opposites.

light	young
find	soft
open	full
hard	lose
old	low
empty	close
high	dark

12. Draw a line between the two words that are the same.

happy	speak
gift	present
talk	also
big	large
too	plate
finish	end
dish	glad

Word Attack Skills

One of the disastrous effects of introducing formal reading materials to deaf children prematurely (i.e., when they do not yet have a sufficiently developed vocabulary and sense of language) is that they encounter so many unknown words that they develop the habit of simply ignoring them and using only the few words they do know. In some cases this may be the best approach (when the unknown word is not essential to understanding the meaning of the sentence, or when the unknown word is really a new word). But often deaf children ignore words which are actually in their language repertoire but which are not in their sight vocabulary. It is very important to teach deaf children the habit of examining words carefully instead of giving up when they do not recognize them at sight. If they do this, they will find that some of the words they thought they did not know they really do know, and if the words are really strangers it is better to have tried than to have abdicated from the start. I find it useful to make a distinction between words that are unfamiliar (their meanings are known, but they are not yet in the child's sight vocabulary) and words that are unknown (the child does not know the meanings at all).

We do not really know how children recognize the words that are in their sight vocabulary (probably the same way they recognize people or objects); but in order to attack unfamiliar words, a fairly systematic approach is advisable. There are different word recognition techniques, and the child has to become adept at using them all. Ultimately, children will develop enough versatility and flexibility to know which particular approaches are most appropriate for a given word in a particular context.

Actually, the best way to begin teaching deaf children to examine words carefully is to demonstrate how the various techniques may be applied when the children encounter words they do not recognize at sight in the transition from informal to formal reading. In this way, the teacher knows that the children actually are acquainted with the "unknown" words, and that word attack skills will actually help. As the children hesitate over a word, the teacher can encourage them to use the appropriate techniques. Generally, it is helpful to proceed from the broadest to the most discrete techniques, but this will depend, of course, on the particular word under attack.

For example, when one group of children read the book their teacher had made about "The Candy Apples That Tasted Awful," they needed help with some of the words. The first sentence was: *Steven brought us apples and Jelly Apple mix.* The teacher could point out the similarities and differences between two often confused words:　　　b　ought
　　　　　　　　　　　br　ought

In this sentence, *We put sticks into the apples.,* the children were encouraged to use a picture clue for the word *sticks.* In the sentence, *We put butter on the cookie paper.,* the teacher covered the second half of the word to help children find *but* in *butter.* In the sentence *Ms. P forgot to turn off the stove and the candy mixture burned!,* the teacher showed the children the similarity between the familiar word

　　　pic　ture, and the word they were attacking:
　　　mix　ture

Until the children gain facility in using the various word recognition skills, the process can be cumbersome and hinder the reading. It is helpful, therefore, to isolate the component word attack skills and provide exercises for drill in using each approach.

1. **Picture Clues.** The child supplies the missing word (orally or by writing) using the picture.

Mary wants something to _____ .

Johnny fell off his bike. He hurt his _____ .

The _____ lives in a barn.

The boy lives in a _____ .

2. **Context Clues.** To use context clues, children must use all the other words in the sentence to figure out the unfamiliar word. This may mean associating to a key word, responding to linguistic clues (position of the word in the sentence, markers—at this stage this response is at unconscious level, if at all), bringing experience and knowledge to bear.

Choose a word for each sentence.

(a.)   brothers   rubbers   neighbors   friends
        circus   laughed   bone   family

Jack gave his dog a _____ .

Mary put on her _____ because it was raining.

John _____ at the funny clown.

There were clowns, horses, and lions at the _____ .

Mother, father, brother, sister—the whole _____ went to the movies.

Mary and Pat play together. They are _____ .

Tom and Dick live next door to each other. They are _____ .

Bob and Steven have the same mother and father. They are _____ .

(b.) bought   was   clown
      brought   saw   brown
                                 down

The boy fell _____ .

We saw a _____ at the circus.

Mary's shoes are _____ .

Mary went to the store. She _____ a new doll.

Mary _____ her doll to school.

John _____ a big dog.

The dog _____ brown and white.

3. **Configuration Clues.** Although a fairly primitive and not terribly effective approach, it is a useful technique for very young children. It involves simply looking at the general length and shape of a word and helps to prevent wild guessing based on no clues. For example, if the child knows that the unfamiliar word is the name of a zoo animal, configuration clues would eliminate some words and narrow down the guessing. If it's a long word, lion and fox would be eliminated, but it could still be elephant or kangaroo or hippopotamus.

4. **Special Features.** This too is a fairly primitive approach; the main purpose is to lead children to develop the habit of examining words carefully instead of guessing wildly. Often young children—and particularly deaf children who are acute observers—do actually get to know words by some distinctive feature within the word. So, if the field were narrowed down to an animal with a long name, chances are that the children can recognize the word

hippopotamus from all the *p*'s interrupting the otherwise flat configuration; they also generally recognize the word *kangaroo* from the *roo* ending.

5. **Known Parts.** As soon as they catch on to this technique, children generally use it enthusiastically. They delight in looking for small words within bigger words; for example, finding *bow* in *bowl, rainbow, bowling.* This approach often helps break children away from casually glancing at the word as a whole, and encourages them to look more closely at words. This habit will be very useful later on, when children begin to syllabify words and to use structural analysis of roots, prefixes, and suffixes. It can, however, be overused by young children and they may become fixated on it. The teacher should encourage them to use other techniques, especially when this approach is actually misleading (for example, finding *at* in *station* is a distractor, and the teacher will have to call attention to the familiar *tion* ending instead).

6. **Word Families.**   This approach helps children to see the similarities among different words, and to appreciate how a small change in a word can produce a big change in meaning. Various manipulative devices can be used to enable children to match words and pictures.

a. For this game, cut two circles of the same size from oaktag. On one of the circles print the word family (i.e., *all*) and cut out a pie section. This will be the outside section. Divide the other circle into as many segments as there will be words and in each segment illustrate the word. This will be the middle section. Make one more circle, slightly larger than the other two. Around the outer rim write the initial letters of each word in the word family. This

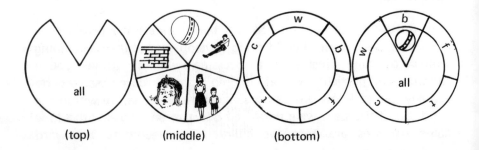

(top)   (middle)   (bottom)

is the bottom circle. Fasten all three circles together loosely in the middle so that they can be rotated by the children.

b. Make a small chart rack and hang strips of oaktag from it, using big rings. Hang narrow strips with just initial letters on each strip (e.g., b, c, l, m, r, t). Then hang a strip with the word family on it (e.g., *ake*). Then hang strips with pictures for the words (e.g., bake, cake, lake, make, rake, take). The children should be able to flip over the strips and match the words to the pictures. This device can also be used with final letters (e.g., b, p, n, t).

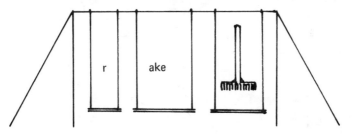

7. **Phonics.** This approach involves teaching children to "sound out" in order to relate the graphemic symbol to the phonological symbol. Even with hearing children, this approach has provoked a great deal of controversy. People who favor the phonics approach argue that it increases independence in word recognition, helps spelling, and encourages correct pronunciation. Those opposed claim that the English language is largely non-phonetic, that children are better off learning to read in larger units, that phonetic analysis stresses the form rather than the meaning of words, and that such emphasis may cause comprehension to suffer.

With deaf children there is even more reason to question how useful a phonics approach can be. However, with children who are taught by the oral-aural system, phonics frequently becomes part of the speech program. As a reading skill, it certainly encourages careful examination of word elements. Teaching primary children to use phonics clues generally includes training them to observe initial letters, final letters, rhyme, blends and digraphs and variations in vowel sounds. Some simple work may be done along these lines with the young deaf child; on the whole, however, it may be a better approach to use with those children with usable residual hearing and with children beyond the primary level.

The following are examples of types of exercises that might be used with some deaf primary children.

a) Mary wants to play with her d _____.

Johnny wants to ride his b _____.

Sally has a pet _____t.

Mother gave Mary a new s _____.

Father gave Mary a new _____s.

b) Draw a circle around all the pictures that have the same beginning sound as:

c) Draw a circle around all the pictures that end with the
    same sound as:

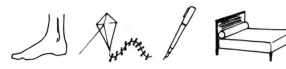

d) What foods are these?

    _____m and eggs

    __m_____ and bacon

    m_____ and spaghetti

    What numbers are these?

    t _____

    ____t____

    _____t

e) Make it rhyme.

     I saw a _____.

     She was very _____.

     May I _____

     In your _____?

Cats are clean.

Grass is _____.

f) Write the first letter of the word under each picture. Then do what it tells you.

_____ _____ _____ _____ _____

8. **Structural Clues.** Analyzing words to find the root and separate it from prefixes and suffixes of various kinds is a more advanced skill, usually developed at later stages. Some simple work with this technique is also suitable and helpful for some primary children.

(a.)   Baby   Bobby   Mother

_____ is not *big*.

Bobby is *bigger* than _____.

Mother is *bigger* than _____.

_____ is the *biggest*.

(b.) Draw a line under the parts of the words that are the same.

eating   sewing   playing   waiting

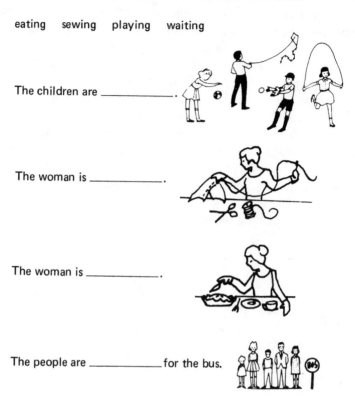

The children are _____ .

The woman is _____ .

The woman is _____ .

The people are _____ for the bus.

Even after children develop the habit of appropriately using word attack skills to figure out unfamiliar words, it still takes time and interrupts the reading. It is important that words that were tediously figured out become sight words so that the child is not repeating the laborious process over and over again. The child's sight vocabulary should be large enough (and constantly growing) to make it possible to read in thought units.

Phrase Reading

It has often been noted that deaf children are generally "word readers," and it takes a very long time before they begin to read in thought units. Of course this is primarily due to the fact that it takes a very long time for them to develop linguistic competence. It may also be due to the fact that in perceiving spoken language visually, they usually pick out key words and use non-verbal clues (gestures, facial expressions, situational constraints) to build in the structural meanings that link these words together. It takes a long time before they can use the structural clues provided by the words and their arrangement in the sentence.

However, it seems to me that teachers of the deaf sometimes inadvertently reinforce the habit of word reading by continuously illustrating the concrete lexical items in a written communication. The selections below illustrate exactly what happens when the child reads words instead of thoughts. These two sentences show almost exactly how the deaf child reads, including the use of a second and misleading meaning for the word *saw*. Unfortunately, too often the integrated picture (at the far right) is never formed.

A cat looked out the window.

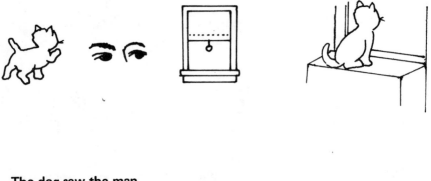

The dog saw the man.

Adapted with permission of the publisher from READING LABORATORY 1a, 1961 edition by Don H. Parker and Genevieve Scannell.
Copyright © 1961 by Science Research Associates, Inc.

One of the steps in building up the habit of fusing discrete word meanings into wholes that are different from the sum of the parts is to promote reading in phrases. Some examples follow.

a) Circle the right picture

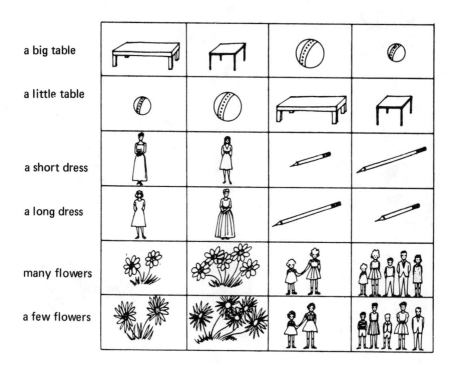

| a big table |
| a little table |
| a short dress |
| a long dress |
| many flowers |
| a few flowers |

b) Match the picture to the phrase. It is much better to do this in a format other than a worksheet. For example, put all the pictures up on the blackboard ledge and briefly show one phrase at a time (written on strips of oaktag). The children vie for who can find the right picture with the briefest exposure. Another technique is to use a tachistoscope and flash the phrase for a short, timed exposure. The children then draw the picture. The point is not really to build up speed reading, but introducing a time factor somehow forces the fusion of the visual image in response to the words.

four rabbits	three dogs	for a girl
two balloons	three ducks	for a boy
two balls	a birthday cake	for a baby
many balloons	a birthday present	many children

c) Draw what's missing.

a big ball and two little balls

a boy between two girls

a cat under a table

Mary is bigger than John.

d) Draw a line to the right word.

It cuts   umbrella
It grows   grass
It's good to eat   sled
for the rain   pie
for the snow   scissors

e) The teacher gradually transforms a word into a complex or compound sentence by adding one part to another (using strips of oaktag). The children draw the picture, changing it appropriately from stage to stage.

A boy   A boy and a girl   A boy and a girl are running.
A boy and a girl are running to meet their father.

A cat   A cat and a dog   A cat and a dog are jumping.
A cat and a dog are jumping over a pile of leaves.

A woman   A woman in a black-and-white skirt   A woman in a black-and-white skirt and a pink blouse   A woman in a black-and-white skirt and a pink blouse with red polka dots   A woman in a black-and-white skirt and a pink blouse with red polka dots is smoking a cigarette.   A woman in a black-and-white skirt and a pink blouse with red polka dots is smoking a cigarette and talking on the telephone.

Sentence Reading

To further develop deaf children's ability to read in thought units, they need practice in grasping the essence of a sentence. Different sentences make different demands on the reader's comprehension. Sometimes sentences offer concrete information in the form of facts or details to be grasped (and later connected to other information). Sometimes the sentence describes a feeling or action which the reader must visualize. Sometimes sentences give directions for doing something. Sometimes sentences present ideas that are more or less abstract. Samples of various kinds follow.

a) Do what the sentences tell you.

Jump three times.
Write your birthday on the blackboard.

Close your left eye.
Clap your hands over your head.

Clap your hands,
And turn around,
Clap your hands,
And bow to the ground.
Touch your head,
And touch your chin,
Open the door
And tiptoe in.

b) Playing charades. Write sentences (or paragraphs) on folded slips of paper. The child picks a slip and carries out the action.

Take off your left shoe.

Pretend you're an old woman.

Put on your hat and coat and go for a walk.

Father was shaving. He cut himself.

Mother is cooking dinner. The telephone rings and she answers it. She talks a long time. The dinner burns.

c) Write sentences on slips of paper and insert them in an envelope pasted on the cover of a magazine. The child finds the pictures in the magazine that illustrate the sentences and cuts them out. The sentences can range from simple and concrete to abstract and complex.

A man is wearing a green hat.

A girl is crying because her doll is broken.

A crowd of people are waiting for a bus.

The sun is peeping out from behind a black cloud.

It's a beautiful spring day.

The man and the woman love each other.

d) Make the sentences true. (Encourage the children to try changing the sentence in different ways by changing different words.)

A bear has five feet.

Milk is green.

The sun shines at night.

Wool comes from cows.

Friday comes before Thursday.

All girls have blue eyes.

e) Following directions.

Color the boat blue.
Color the ball green and white.
Color the apple red.

Color one ball yellow.
Color two balls green.
Color the fourth ball red.

Draw a table.
Draw a black cat under the table.
Cut out a ball.
Color it green and yellow.
Paste it on the table.

Draw a line under the apple.
Put an X on the ball.
Draw a circle around the boat.

Draw a line over the small boat.
Draw a circle around two balls.
Put an X over the first big boat.

Draw a line under the house with the chimney.
Put an X on the cat under the chair.

Put an X on the girl who is playing ball.
Draw a circle around the boy who is riding his bicycle.
Draw a line under the girl who is jumping rope.
Draw a line over the one who has a kite.

Draw a line under something you use when it rains.
Put an X on the thing that is the fastest.
Draw a circle around something you see in the sky at night.
Put an X over the thing that goes on water.

Draw a cloud over the house.
Draw a line under the one who is riding a bicycle.
Draw a ball for the small girl.
Put an X on the animal that barks.
Draw a line from the second tree to the house.
Draw a bird in the third tree.
Color the big girl's dress green.
Draw a circle around the animal that can climb a tree.
Put an X under the tree that is nearest the house.

Paragraph Reading

For the primary deaf child, reading in longer and longer units presents unbelievable problems and challenges. It requires the integration of all the skills in reading they have been guided to develop through the use of regular and special materials. It is very important that deaf children have an abundance of easy reading materials which are both interesting and within the children's linguistic ability; even without language snares, reading and understanding paragraphs and stories require that the child develop the habit of doing many complex things all at once. It is a little like learning to drive a car; at first each of the mechanical skills involved needs to be developed with intense concentration; with practice and experience these skills become automatic, freeing the driver to concentrate on the larger judgments needed in driving.

As children decode words, they need to fuse them into thought units, forming mental pictures which translate the words into referential meanings. Then the mental image formed by one thought unit is retained in the memory while the next group of words is translated into referential meaning. The two images must now be interrelated. For deaf beginning readers, this is a skill which does not emerge automatically. It must be specifically taught and cultivated.

Phonological coding plays an important role in short-term memory. This may account for the tendency of deaf children, who by and large do not use phonological coding, to treat each sentence as though it were independent of the others in the paragraph.

Just one example might illustrate the point, although teachers of the deaf can undoubtedly supply many examples of this fragmenting process from their own experience. A teacher had given her class the following short story to read and illustrate: *Bobby is riding his green bicycle. He sees a red light. Bobby does not stop. A red car hits Bobby.* One child illustrated each sentence for what was contained in that sentence, without carrying into each successive sentence the information from previous sentences. Thus, Bobby appears on his bicycle only in the illustration for the first sentence; when the car hits Bobby, Bobby is not on his bicycle.

Another example of such fragmentation that I vividly recall comes from an answer on an achievement test. One of the questions following a paragraph about mother cooking a dinner which included a pie was: "For dessert mother made (pie   cake   pudding)." A child who had answered the other questions for the paragraph correctly chose pudding for this answer. When I asked her about it afterwards, she told me that dessert *had* to be pudding. In her experience with school lunches this was generally so; therefore she ignored the information in the paragraph in answering the question.

While the approach of most deaf children to reading may be idiosyncratic, it is rarely thoughtless. In fact, they struggle to bring all they can to bear in interpreting this difficult medium. They are generally forced to do a great deal of guessing in reading since so much of the language is unknown to them, and they use all their thinking skill, acuity as visual observers, and their experience, in trying to interpret the printed word. That is why it is so important that we try to provide them with teacher-made materials with known language that will enable them to successfully build up their reading techniques. Simple stories and activities should be provided to develop the skills needed in reading in longer units—visualizing, integrating one thought unit with another, reading beyond the words, organizing main ideas and their supporting details, anticipating, and remembering.

a) Visualizing sequences:

Write a paragraph on the board. Cover it and have the children dramatize the action in its proper sequence.

Mother was busy cleaning the house. First, she washed the clothes and hung them out to dry. Then she washed the dishes, dried them and put them away. After that, she made the beds. Then she vacuumed the rugs and dusted the furniture.

Mary went to the store with her mother. She tried on a pair of shoes. She walked around. They were too small. They hurt. She tried on another pair. They were too big. She tried on another pair. They were just right. Mother bought them.

Put these sentences in the right order, so that they tell a story:

She was afraid.
She ran home.
She saw a big dog.
Mary went for a walk.

She bought flour, eggs and milk.
The family ate it for supper.
Mrs. Jones went to the grocery store.
She baked a cake.

A glass fell off the table and broke.
He jumped on the table.
The cat hid behind a chair.
The cat saw a ball on the table.

Mother was angry.
The dog ate the cake.
She put it on the table to cool.
Mother baked a cake.

She went to the kitchen.
Her brother changed the program.
Susan was watching The Munsters.
Susan was surprised to see Batman.
She wanted something to drink.
She scolded her brother.

When you present children with a story to be illustrated, care must be taken that you are not contributing to their tendency to fragment the separate details (as in the Bobby on his bicycle story) by asking them to draw a picture for each sentence. Sometimes it is helpful to indicate how many pictures they should draw; this may help them perceive the thought, action or idea units. But sometimes the teacher should leave it up to the children to decide how many pictures should be drawn. And sometimes the teacher should require that the whole story be recapitulated in just one composite picture. Whatever children draw, the teacher should watch to see that they are reading between the lines and making good inferences by encouraging them to put into their pictures details that are implicit but not stated in the story. For example, in the Bobby and his bicycle story, Bobby is apparently riding in the street and the child should draw an appropriate background setting.

Read the story and illustrate it. Draw six pictures.

> Janet wanted to buy a present for her mother for her birthday. She took her money out of her piggy bank and went to the store. She saw many pretty things, but she did not have enough money to buy any of them. She walked back home very sadly. On the way home, she saw a cute little kitten. It had no home. Janet felt so sorry for the kitten. Then she had a wonderful idea. She took the kitten home and put it in a box. She gave it to Mother for her birthday.

> Richard found a dog in the street. The dog had no home. Richard felt sorry for the dog. He took the dog home. But Mother said "NO! I do not want a dog in this house. The dog must go." Richard was sad. He took the dog up to his room and hid him under his bed. That night when everybody was sleeping, a robber tried to get into the house through the window. The dog barked and barked. The robber ran away. Mother kissed Richard. "That's a good dog," she said. "That dog can stay."

Read the story and illustrate it. Draw as many pictures as you like.

> Bobby got a new toy boat for Christmas. He loved it and wanted to play with it right away. He went upstairs to the bathroom and locked the door. He turned on the water in the bathtub, and put his new boat in the water. Soon there was enough water in the tub. Bobby wanted to turn the water off so he could play with his boat. But he couldn't. He tried and tried, but the water went all over the floor. Bobby screamed. Mother and Father came running up. But they could not open the door! Father had to get a hammer and break the lock.

It was snowing! Jose and Mike were so happy. They went out to play in the snow. They rode on their sleds. They had a snowball fight. Then they made a big, beautiful snowman. But it was sunny out. They were afraid that their beautiful snowman would melt. They wanted to keep him. Then they thought of a good idea. They carried their snowman into their house and put it in the freezer. After supper, Mother went to get some ice cream from the freezer. Guess what she saw!

Sometimes the teacher may give the children the beginning of a story and instead of (or in addition to) having them draw the whole story, they might be asked to just draw their own ending.

Draw what happened next.

Mother had a lot of work to do in the house. She put the baby in the playpen with a lot of toys. Then Mother went into the kitchen. She washed the dishes and cooked supper. Then she went upstairs to clean. Suddenly she heard a loud noise. She ran downstairs and looked in the playpen. The baby was gone!

Roger was walking to school one day. He stopped at the corner for a red light. He saw that there was something on the ground in the middle of the street. When the light changed, Roger started to cross the street. He bent down and picked up the thing he saw. It was a wallet!

Mary's mother told her to go to the store to buy some milk. Mother gave Mary a dollar. Mary put it in her pocket. On the way to the store, Mary sneezed. She took a handkerchief out of her pocket to cover her nose. Mary bought the milk in the store. She took it to the cashier. She put her hand in her pocket to get the dollar. There was the handkerchief, but no dollar!

b) Drawing inferences. To build up the skill of reading beyond the words, it is helpful to present short exercises in which children can draw specific inferences based on given facts and details.

(1) Mary's mother sent her to the store to buy some milk. Mary went to _____ . (the pet shop, the grocery store, the tailor)

(2) Jane and Sally asked mother if they could go to the movies. Mother said all right, and gave Jane money for both of them. Jane and Sally are _____ . (friends, sisters, cousins) Who is older? _____ . (Jane, Sally)

(3) It was feeding time at the _____. The lions ate their meat. The seals ate their fish. The elephants ate their hay. The monkeys ate their bananas.

(4) John wanted to use his new sled. Each morning he looked out to see if it was _____. One day when he looked out he saw big white snowflakes. He was so _____.

(5) Johnny saw a woman carrying many packages. She dropped one. Johnny picked it up.

Who said:
>"You're welcome."
>"Thank you."
>"May I help you?"

(6) Johnny was walking to school. He stopped to play with a dog on the street. Then he saw that it was late. What do you think he did?
>He cried.
>He ran.
>He went home.

(7) Riddles of all kinds.

>I am red outside and white inside. I grow on a tree. I am good to eat. I am _____.

>You can ride in me. But you can only go up and down. You cannot go forwards or backwards. I am _____.

>I am made of glass. When you look in me, you will see yourself. I am _____.

c) Choosing titles for paragraphs provides good practice in helping the child get the main idea of a selection. For example:

The children were so happy to see the snow. They couldn't wait to go outdoors. Mary wanted to go sled riding. Bob and Jack wanted to have a snowball fight. Peter wanted to make a snowman.

The best title for the story is:
>Winter on the Farm
>A Snowman
>A Snowball Fight
>Fun in the Snow

Mother said, "What do you want for your birthday?" Juanita said, "A pet."

Mother said, "Do you want a kitten?" "No," said Juanita, "a kitten will scratch me."

"Do you want a dog?" asked Mother. "No," said Juanita. "I do not want to walk a dog."

"Do you want a bird?" asked Mother. "No," said Juanita. "I cannot hug a bird."

"Then do you want a rabbit? A rabbit will not scratch you. You do not have to walk a rabbit. And you can hug a rabbit," said Mother. "Oh, yes," said Juanita. "I would like a rabbit for a pet."

The best title for the story is:

No Dogs for Juanita   A Birthday Present
Choosing a Pet   A Rabbit

d) Following Directions. This requires careful, precise reading of a sequence of details. It often also involves knowing some specialized language. The best way to build up this skill is through directions for actually making or doing things. This is not only highly motivational, but self-checking. If you make a mistake, the thing doesn't turn out right and you have to go back and read more carefully. Directions for games, for sewing, cooking, can be adapted to the primary level.

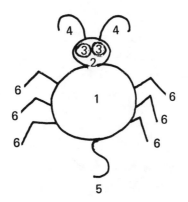

(1)

> This is Cootie.
> He has a body.
> He has a head.
> He has two eyes.
> He has two feelers
> He has a tail.
> And he has six legs.

HOW TO PLAY COOTIE

Each player must have a piece of paper and a pencil.

Choose for 1st, 2nd, 3rd, etc.

When it is your turn, throw the die.

First, you must get one.

If you don't get one, you will try again when it is your turn again.

If you get one, draw Cootie's body on your paper.

When it is your turn again, you must get two.

If you do not get two, you will try again on your next turn.

If you do get two, draw Cootie's head on your paper.

Then try to get three. If you get three, draw Cootie's eyes.

If you do not get three, try again next time.

Then try to get four. When you get four, draw Cootie's feelers.

Then try to get five. When you get five, draw Cootie's tail.

Then try to get six. When you get six, draw Cootie's legs.

If you get to six first, you win!

(2) Make a Spinner

> You will need:
>
> > a piece of cardboard
> > a round plastic lid
> > crayons or paints or magic markers
> > scissors
> > a toothpick

Put the plastic lid on the piece of cardboard and trace all around it with a crayon.

Cut out the circle.

Draw a design on it.

Stick the toothpick through the middle of the circle.

Hold the toothpick at the top and spin it.

(3) A Trick

Can you tie a knot in a piece of string without letting go of either end?

Here's how to do it:
Put the string on a table. Let the two ends hang over one side of the table.

Cross your arms on your chest. Put your left hand on top of your right arm. Then weave your right hand over your left arm and then under your left armpit.

Keep your arms crossed this way and pick up the two ends of the string with your two hands.

Hold the string in your hands and unfold your arms.

Language Through Reading

In addition to all the new vocabulary, certain language constructions appear even in beginning reading matter that will be difficult for deaf children. Drill in these forms can be helpful:

(1) Can - Cannot	A bird can fly.	Right	Wrong
	A fish cannot swim.	Right	Wrong
	A cat can sing.	Right	Wrong
	A baby cannot read.	Right	Wrong
(2) All - Some	All girls have curly hair.	Right	Wrong
	Some girls have short hair.	Right	Wrong
	All children have ten toes.	Right	Wrong
	Some dogs have five legs.	Right	Wrong

(3) Always - Never

Christmas is always in December.	Right	Wrong
Leaves are always green.	Right	Wrong
Thanksgiving is never on Monday.	Right	Wrong
It never rains in the summer.	Right	Wrong

(4) Each - All - Every

Draw a ring around all the cats.

Draw a ring around each dog.

Draw a line under every animal that flies.

(5) Subject - Object

Put an X on the right picture.

The girl took a picture of the man.

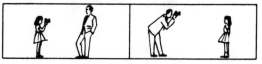

Mary gave Dick a lollipop.

(6) Compounds

Mary has a green-and-yellow dress.

Dick has a brown dog and a black dog.

(7) Prepositions. Draw a line from the words to the right picture.

something to write with

something to write on

a present for mother

a present from mother

She ran in the room.

She ran into the room.

They walked to the park.

They walked in the park.

Beginning Dictionary Skills

Although the primary deaf child is not ready to use the dictionary to look up meanings of unknown words, it is helpful to introduce the dictionary as a reference source, and to acquaint children with its organization and use on a simple level. Picture dictionaries are used at this stage. The first independent use children will make of dictionaries will be to look up the spelling of a word they want to write. To do this, the children must be taught the various skills that will enable them to locate the word systematically and expeditiously, instead of leafing through the dictionary randomly.

1. The first thing to know is the alphabet. Singing the alphabet song and playing alphabet games help with rote memory. For example: Everybody stands up; the teacher points to one child after another to name the successive letters. A child who misses has to sit down. Everybody who is still standing when you get to z wins. The goal is to have everybody still standing. Or, the teacher writes the letters of the alphabet on large cards and attaches strings long enough to go over the children's heads on the cards. Children are given the cards at random, and they hang them around their necks. Then they arrange themselves in alphabetic order across the room.

2. Children have to have real facility with the sequence of the letters in the alphabet so that they do not constantly have to recite the whole thing to get to the particular letter they need. Exercises like these are helpful:

What's missing?	h i _ k l
What comes next?	e f g h _
What comes after <u>r</u>?	
What comes before <u>p</u>?	

3. Children need to relate the name of the letter to the sound of the letter, and to its written symbol. Teacher and child play this game using alphabet blocks (or plastic letters). Teacher gives a sound, child gives the name and finds the block. Teacher gives a letter name, child gives the sound and finds the block. Child gives the name, teacher gives the sound and finds the block. Child gives the sound, teacher gives the name and finds the block. Teacher makes mistakes sometimes for the child to catch.

4. Figuring out what letter a word begins with is a skill that takes much practice. It requires isolating the initial sound and relating the written symbol to that sound (and, of course, with some of the

erratic spellings in English this can be very tough; such words should be avoided as much as possible at the beginning, until alternate spellings for sounds are learned). The exercises suggested for beginning phonics work are very appropriate for dictionary work. For example, put up a great many pictures in collage-like fashion. Ask children to find all the words that begin with *p, k,* etc.

The game Grandfather's Chest gives excellent practice with the alphabet and with beginning sounds of words. In this game the carrier sentence: *I went to the store and I bought...* is used by each player in turn, with each player repeating everything said by the previous players and adding an item beginning with the next letter. Children who have good vocabularies might stick to one category and see how far they can take it (e.g., I went to the grocery and I bought: an apple, a banana, a cake, a doughnut, some eggs, etc.).

5. Giving children some practice doing their own alphabetizing is helpful. Start with letters in sequence, then letters in skipped sequence, then words in sequence, words in skipped sequence, and finally words with the same initial letter.

Put in alphabetical order:

m j o n l k   _____

s c v p h t   _____

Kathy Ida Maria Harry Louis Juan   _____ _____ _____ _____ _

giraffe bear zebra lion tiger elephant   _____ _____ _____ _____

Charles Catherine Clark Cynthia Craig Connie   _____ _____ ____

6. Just before children are ready to use the dictionary to find out how to write a word they need, a demonstration should show them how to estimate whether the word will be toward the beginning, middle, or back of the dictionary. Using riddles makes it more exciting. Compose your own riddles so that you are fairly sure the children will know the answer but will not know how to spell it. Give two children picture dictionaries and see who can be first to find the word and write it. Later you can point out that it's faster if you figure out approximately where in the dictionary the word would be, and more efficient if you make a stab at the second letter as well.

If I want to know the time, I look at the clock. If I want to know the date, I look at the _____ .

When I am sick, I go to the doctor. When I have a toothache, I go to the _____ .

The playroom has lots of toys. The ＿＿＿＿＿＿ has lots of books.

The mailman brings you letters. The ＿＿＿＿＿＿ helps you when you're lost.

It looks like a horse, but it lives in the zoo. It has black and white stripes. It is a ＿＿＿＿＿＿ .

Apples, pears, and bananas are fruits. Carrots, peas, and beans are

＿＿＿＿＿＿ .

If deaf children are to be able to cope with the problems that lie ahead of them, they must, during their primary years, acquire a solid foundation in terms of language, concepts, and reading skills and habits. The gap between deaf children's actual language level and the language level of reading materials widens beyond the primary level. Although reading may be used as a source for language teaching, unless children are given an abundance of material with language known to them that they can read on their own, they will not succeed in mastering the skills that are appropriate and necessary at the primary level. This will add the burden of deficient reading skills to the inevitable burden of deficient language. It will make reading a frustrating task and destroy motivation. The teacher has to be both flexible and knowledgeable to prevent such a disastrous outcome. ☐

DEVELOPMENTAL ACTIVITIES:

5. Intermediate

Generally, the intermediate level spans the ages from 9 to 12. It is very difficult to apply the grade level designations used with hearing children to deaf children because not only is the academic progress of deaf children necessarily slower, it is also very uneven. Over and above the typical spread of individual differences are differences from subject to subject, with deaf children doing most poorly in language-based subjects, as is to be expected, and best in areas relatively language-independent (e.g., math). Nevertheless, a general description of the work at this level could include the expectation that it would cover third and fourth grade reading for most children. There will, of course, be children who will, even at intermediate ages, be continuing with primary skills. Just as during these pre-teen years physical growth styles manifest wide variations, so too do cognitive styles.

From my point of view this is the most difficult level of all, presenting the greatest problems and challenges. An unfortunate combination of developmental factors converges to make this a trying time. During a period when the most extraordinary academic demands are made, children are so absorbed in their own social and emotional growth and inner turmoil that academic motivation is at a low ebb. Where the transition into formal reading was gentle for primary children, the passage into the intermediate level is abrupt. The concrete vocabulary and simple sentence structure of primary reading materials, which were far below the linguistic level of the hearing child, were admirably suited for the deaf child. The much more complicated and abstract vocabulary and sentence structure of intermediate materials closes the gap between the oral and written language levels of the hearing child. Yet it creates an enormous chasm between the language deaf children "know" and the language they are supposed to read. Even if the lexical items were largely known to the deaf child (which they are not), it would be difficult to understand the written sentence without responding to grammatic clues.

To add to the burdens, whereas primary children were guided to acquire new language and concepts through carefully planned experiences and activities, intermediate children are expected to take more responsibility for their own learning, and to learn independently as well as vicariously. The primary level is traditionally characterized as the level of "learning to read," and the intermediate level as "reading to learn." Having a good background of language and experience, hearing children should now be ready to use reading to learn new ideas and information and expand their concepts. But how can deaf children learn new ideas through reading if the language itself is new to them? At the primary level, unknown language interfered with learning to read; at the intermediate level, deaf children continue the struggle to learn to read while at the same time struggling to learn new language; now they must add to this complicated process the learning of new concepts through reading. Is it any wonder that the rate of progress is painfully slow at this level? This is a sorry fact that teachers, parents, and pupils at this level have to live with at the same time that they exert every effort to overcome it. The dilemma "good readers have good language—but good language is necessary to be a good reader" is never so apparent as at the intermediate level.

Aims

The general goal is to establish the habit and ability to read a wide range of material independently for pleasure and information. To achieve this goal, specific competencies must be fostered:

1. Decoding word meanings—The materials at this level make

enormous demands on children to both broaden and deepen their vocabularies. This involves:

a) an ever and rapidly expanding sight vocabulary.

b) an interest and approach to words that encourage the careful and mature examination of words and their elements, analyzing, comparing and generalizing observed details; storing new words in the child's linguistic memory bank to be retrieved when needed.

c) a beginning ability to use techniques for analyzing unknown words—some independence in learning new language through reading.

2. Literal comprehension

a) Reading in thought units involves the ability to handle complicated sentence constructions and grasping (consciously or unconsciously) the kernel sentences underlying complex-compound surface structures.

b) Reading in longer units involves following a logical or chronological sequence of actions, details and ideas. Organizing parts into wholes, giving the various elements proportional importance, makes it much easier to remember what you are reading.

3. Understanding the differences between different kinds of materials builds individual taste in selecting independent reading materials and encourages the use of different techniques in reading for different purposes and for different reading matter. At the intermediate level, textbooks are generally introduced into the curriculum, and children must be taught how to handle math, science, and social science books.

4. Reading creatively means using good habits of thinking while reading, seeing relationships, drawing inferences, and exercising personal judgment in evaluating the impact of the material.

The Program

The problems are great, the demands exacting. To meet them requires a diversified program and a versatile teacher. Reading instruction is not restricted to the 45 minutes of the reading period but goes on all day long. The teacher has somehow to ease the burden on the pupils by setting specific limited goals for specific activities and not trying to achieve everything at once. At this stage, the only material the children will be reading that is not beyond their linguistic abilities will be that specifically created by the teacher (rewrites of standard materials, skill-building exercises, blackboard and functional writing). Everything else will require the learning of new language along with the learning of new ideas. The teacher has to recognize that even if the children have reading skills that are appropriate for their age level, the added burdens render these skills only minimally effective. Thus, the teacher has to accept and applaud limited performance, provided it is the best for that child with that material.

The three facets of the reading program—the promotion of specific reading skills, the teaching of new language through reading, and the learning of new ideas through reading—may at times merge and at other times be separated. The diagnostic skill of the teacher, on which hinges the selection and use of different materials, will determine to a large extent whether or not the program is frustrating. If the teacher limits the goal to moving each pupil along in each of the three reading areas at a realistic rate, the reading program can be interesting and rewarding. It is always good for teachers to keep in mind that if they do little more than sustain a high interest in reading at this level, this in itself will be an enormous contribution. It will keep children from giving up on books, and when the children's linguistic ability catches up with their reading interests it will be much smoother sailing. So it is up to the teacher to make each reading experience as easy and as successful as possible by separating out the goals and by using different materials for different purposes. Keeping very good records on each child helps considerably.

The specific reading period may be devoted one day (or more) to the reading of a story in a basal reader, other days to work in the weekly periodical or in library books, or to skill-building or remedial exercises. It may be conducted in a group, or with individual children. It may be culminated in written exercises to test comprehension and memory of what was read, or by a follow-up activity (e.g., a dramatic presentation), or by teacher-made exercises to meet specific observed needs.

In addition to the work during the reading period, children will be engaged in functional reading, reading in relation to other curriculum activities, and free-choice reading. Whenever children are doing supervised reading of any kind, they should be observed and encouraged to use the best reading skills of which they are capable. And they should be helped to use reading for language and conceptual growth by having an adult available to fill in the gaps. In other words, whenever children are reading, guide them when that is needed, and hold them responsible for reading on their own when that is possible.

It is important that the program of reading *to* children be continued at the intermediate level. Even though the teacher will be easing the burdens on the children by explaining and teaching unknown language, developmental reading is necessarily slow and arduous. There will be many books that intermediate children would be very much interested in but would find too difficult for independent reading. These are the kinds of books the teacher could advantageously read to the class.

The exercises and activities that follow illustrate some of the skills to be developed at the intermediate level. It is not only through drills such as these that the skills are developed, but through all the developmental, functional, and remedial reading activities.

Vocabulary

Every effort must be made to keep the children's known vocabulary abreast of the reading vocabulary. In view of the fact that new words come up with overwhelming frequency, and that many of these words are abstract and difficult, this requires rigorous application. The teacher must attempt to weave into all class activities as much meaningful repetition of new vocabulary items as possible. However, since deaf children cannot possibly get as much or as easy exposure to new words as hearing children, the teacher has to compensate for the quantitative deficiency by the quality of the teaching. New vocabulary and language forms must be presented with great impact so that they leave a vivid impression. It is not enough simply to define new words; connotations and shades of meaning, as well as denotive, precise meanings, should be explored. The word should be classified with other words in the same category and differentiated from other words that have subtly different or grossly contrasted meanings. Variations of the word form and their operation in sentences should be pointed out. The more varied the associations and the richer the clues, the more likely is the new word to be remembered and become part of the children's language repertoire.

Intermediate children, like primary children, should have a temporary and a permanent system for recording new language. I used to have children tape a piece of paper to their desks at the beginning of each week. Children were encouraged to develop the habit of jotting down any new word, idiom, or expression that came up (in reading or in any other activity). Often the same words appeared on all the children's lists, but some words appeared only on certain children's lists. At the end of the week children transferred these words and expressions to a permanent recording system. At the primary level, the special device for this purpose was maintaining one group set of booklets or boxes arranged in categories. At the intermediate level, each child maintains a separate vocabulary book in which the new entries are recorded both alphabetically and in other listings (e.g., synonyms, antonyms, homonyms, multiple meanings, idioms, foreign words, slang). The richer and more varied the associations, the more likely are the new items to be remembered. (For example, suppose the word *seize* came up; it would be recorded and defined under *s,* and also in the section on homonyms with *sees* and *seas,* and in the section on synonyms with *grab.*)

Vocabulary games and exercises can perform very important functions. If they are interesting and enough fun they will be played over and over again, thus providing the repetition needed to incorporate the new words into the children's sight vocabulary. In addition, formal and informal word study activities can intensify children's awareness and versatility in analyzing words. Word play can be entertaining; it can also be informative. Children can improve their word attack skills and become more proficient word guessers. The suggestions that follow are samples of techniques that can be adapted by the teacher to provide needed practice with relevant vocabulary. Additional ideas for both intermediate and advanced levels may be found in word game and puzzle books, such as:

Arnold, H and B. Lee, *Jumble.* New York: Signet, NAL, 1967.

Crawford, J., *Hooray for Play.* New York: Doubleday, 1959.

84 Rebus Games. New York: Hart, 1976.

Espy, W.R., *An Almanac of Words at Play.* New York: Potter, Crown, 1975.

Gardner, M., *Arrow Book of Brain Teasers.* New York: Scholastic Book Services, 1973.

Gardner, M., *Codes, Ciphers and Secret Writing.* New York: Simon & Schuster, 1972.

Gardner, M., *Perplexing Puzzles and Tantalizing Teasers.* New York: Simon & Schuster, 1969.

Hoban, T., *Push Pull, Empty Full.* New York: Macmillan, 1975.

Hurwitz, A., and A. Goddard, *Games to Improve Your Child's English.* New York: Simon & Schuster, 1970.

Kahn, B., *One Day It Rained Cats and Dogs.* New York: Coward, 1965.

Keane, B., *Jest in Pun.* New York: Scholastic, 1966.

Lewis, R., *Pencil Pastimes.* New York: Doubleday, 1957.

Moore, E., *Lucky Book of Riddles.* New York: Scholastic, 1964.

Mosesson, E., N., R., C., C., *The Perfect Put-Down.* New York: Scholastic, 1974.

Nurnberg, M., *Fun With Words.* Englewood Cliffs, N.J.: Prentice Hall, 1970.

Robbins, P. and T. Fenton, *Antics.* New York: Simon & Schuster, 1969.

Rockowitz, M., *Arrow Book of Word Games.* New York: Scholastic Book Services, 1964.

Sage, M., *If You Talked to a Boar.* New York: Macmillan.

Sage, M., *Words Inside Words.* New York: Macmillan.

Steig, W., *C D B!* New York: Simon & Schuster, 1968.

Taylor, M., *Mysticryptics.* Glenview, Ill.: Scott, Foresman, 1971.

White, Mary Sue, *Word Twins.* Nashville, Tenn.: Abingdon, 1961.

Winn, M. and P. Ott, *Riddles, Rhymes and Jokes.* New York: Young Readers Press, 1963.

1. *Concentration*

This game is played exactly as described at the primary level, but instead of matching words and pictures, the children have to match pairs of synonyms, antonyms, or homonyms, or plural forms or past and present verb forms.

2. *Rebus Games*

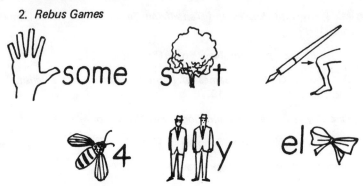

3. *Finding small words in a long word,* e.g., "dictionary"—ran, not, city, train, diary, dairy, try, etc.

4. *Simplified acrostics*

Fill in the blanks. Now take the first letter of each word you put in the blank. This will give you a word which describes summer weather.

The most important female in a story is the (heroine)   _ _ _ _ _ _ _

Shaped like an egg   _ _ _ _ (oval)

You can look at the stars through a (telescope)   _ _ _ _ _ _ _ _ _

5. *Anagrams*

Use the same letters for each word, but change them around.

There are nine players on a baseball   _ _ _ _

A kind of food   _ _ _ _

Not wild   _ _ _ _

A friend   _ _ _ _

What you do when you see a red light   _ _ _ _

The office where you buy stamps   _ _ _ _

A dirt mark   _ _ _ _

Opposite of bottoms   _ _ _ _

Start with the word *at.* Change the letters around and add a letter each time.

What some adults drink   _ _ _

A story   _ _ _ _

A dish   _ _ _ _ _

Mars is a   _ _ _ _ _ _

6. *Categories game.* Fill each box with a word beginning with the letter indicated.

	P	A	B	T	S
Flowers					
Dogs					
Countries					
Cars					
Vegetables					

7. *Analogies*

Yellow is to banana as _____ is to tomato.

Socks are to _____ as gloves are to hands.

Rose is to flower as poodle is to _____.

Oven is to pie as _____ is to ice cream.

_____ is to needle as write is to pencil.

Fell is to fall as _____ is to buy.

8. *Series*

hot cold young old find lose high _____

little small penny cent present gift shut _____

dog animal red color apple fruit spinach _____

cat kitten dog puppy horse pony sheep _____

bird fly fish swim baby crawl soldier _____

man men foot feet story stories child _____

go went throw threw have had think _____

waiter waitress king queen husband wife bride ____

park bark paste baste pull bull pier ____

fat fan met men night nine boat _____

coat kite show shy toad tide note _____

so sew bare bear eight ate right _____

9. *Down Escalator*

Change one letter at a time to make the next word.

I hope you enjoy playing this	g a _ e
Opposite of different	_ a m e
The storekeeper made the prices lower for the	s a _ e
A boy is a	_ a l e
5,280 feet	m _ l e
Something good to drink	m i l _
A beautiful, soft material	_ i l k
Not feeling well	s i _ k
You wear it on your foot	s _ c k
To close with a key	_ o c k
See	l o _ k
Past of take	_ o o k
A hammer is a	t o o _
What a sheep gives	_ o o l
What a pencil is made of	w o o _
The dictionary is full of these	w o _ d
Past of wear	w o r _
That's all there is, there is no	_ o r e

10. *Match the word to the picture*

	chilly	color
	collar	clear

	picture	pitcher
	glass	place

musician

magician

magazine

11. *Draw the picture*

    Insect

    Fist

    Prison

    A bowl of fruit

    A broken window

    A few children

    A hole in a stocking

12. *Cross out the word that doesn't belong*

(a) evening	noon	soon	midnight
(b) cellar	sidewalk	attic	porch
(c) chocolate	vanilla	butter	pistachio
(d) dime	pay	cent	nickel
(e) rubber	leather	plastic	package

13. *Classifying*

(a.)   Put X next to all the words that are names of animals.

       Put Y next to all the words that name parts of animals.

       Put Z next to all the words that tell what animals give.

horse	neck	hen
milk	sheep	feet
ears	head	pony
eggs	wool	tail
cow	pig	meat

(b.)   Put a circle next to all the things you would find in the kitchen.

       Put a check next to all the things you would find in a bedroom.

       Put a cross next to all the things you would find in the bathroom.

oven	pillow	can opener
closet	saucer	sheet
toothbrush	bureau	washcloth
blanket	towel	refrigerator
toaster	medicine chest	shower curtain

14. *Scrambled words*

Tic-tac-toe can be played by two children (or two teams), with players drawing from a deck a card with a scrambled word on it (alone, or in a sentence, or with a definition). If players can write the word correctly, they put an X or O on the tic-tac-toe board.

15. *Rhymes*

Bells ring,
Birds _____ .

Books have pages,
Zoos have _____.

You sit on chairs,
You climb up _____.

A tomato is red,
A corpse is _____ .

Something cold is not hot,
A few is not a _____.

16. *Alphabet*

Under each letter, write the letter that comes next in the alphabet. Then answer the question. Use the same code for writing your answer.

V	G	Z	S	R	X	N	T	Q	E	Z	U	N	Q	H

S	D	H	B	D	B	Q	D	Z	L	E	K	Z	U	N	Q

17. *Commercial materials*

Many boxed and packaged games can be useful in the classroom. For example: Scrabble, Spill and Spell, Password, Down You Go, and Anagrams give children facility with words and can be enjoyed at whatever level of proficiency they may be played.

Vocabulary Scrapbooks   Some of the most delightful home-made materials I have seen have been scrapbooks which record various kinds of vocabulary items accumulated and illustrated by children. These books are not created all at once but are continuous affairs, added to all through the year. As a new word comes up, a booklet is started. For example, suppose the word "tinkle" has come up. After its meaning has been established, a book called "Words That Tell How Things Sound" (or "Onomatopoetic Words"—children get a big kick out of this impressive word) will be started. The word "tinkle" will go in, and any other words the children volunteer for this category (such as "zoom," "roar") will be entered. The book is then hung up in the classroom and whenever another such word is encountered it is added to the book. The same thing happens with other word categories, and soon the class has a library of home-made books which keep growing by timely additions. The teacher can give further currency to these new words by using these books as sources for the words to be used in games and exercises. The books also serve as reference books for the children. Here are some examples of topics for these books:

1. Collecting and illustrating words with multiple meanings.

One teacher did an amusing **"L ☼ ☼ K BOOK"** with her children which included illustrations for: *look up* literally meaning upwards, and *look up* meaning consult a dictionary or other reference; *look up to; look down on; look forward to; look like; look alike; look ahead,* and, as a lark, *look! a head!*

2. Collecting idiomatic expressions; illustrating literal and figurative meanings, e.g.,

At 11:00 p.m. little John was still not asleep. Mary was beside herself.

3. Collecting different expressions with the same meaning, e.g., in a jiffy, in two shakes of a lamb's tail, in a flash, before you can say Jack Robinson.

4. Collecting words suggestive of sound, e.g., buzz, boom, crackle.

5. Collecting picture words, e.g., zig-zag, mammoth, frail.

6. Collecting variations within a word family, e.g., said, remarked, cried, called, whispered, shouted, shrieked, answered, bellowed, exclaimed, announced.

7. Associating adjectives with nouns, e.g., judge—wise; dancer—graceful; peach—fuzzy.

8. Classifying words. Names of flowers, names of cars.

9. Collecting synonyms, antonyms, homonyms.

10. Finding meanings of proper names, e.g., Mathilda—heroine; Bradley—living near a broad lee or field.

11. Tracing simple word origins, e.g., chewing gum—the gum of a tree which could be chewed.

12. Studying prefixes and suffixes, e.g., un, less.

Tackling Unknown Words Children at the intermediate level will constantly be encountering new words in their reading. In some cases, the teacher will simply fill in the unknown meanings, *teaching* language through reading, and freeing the children to read what they can on their own. However, in some cases it is appropriate to help children develop systematic procedures and skills for *independent learning* of language through reading. Using the dictionary would seem to be the logical solution, but this is difficult and interruptive and children need to be taught other steps they can take rather than resorting routinely to the dictionary.

The steps in tackling new words are: 1. identifying the unknown words, 2. using contextual and grammatical clues to guess at the meanings, 3. knowing when and how to use the dictionary. These skills will be more fully developed and enlarged at the advanced level, but some work on this can and should be done at the intermediate level.

Very often deaf children work only with the words they know in the sentence, using these words to guess at the total meaning. Since this is fairly ineffectual with any but the most simple sentences, children must be taught to pay closer attention to unknown words. When students are merely picking out the words they easily recognize, the chances are that they are relying mainly on configuration clues or on the appearance of the word as a whole. This habit must be replaced by the habit of carefully examining parts of words. Often a word that is actually known by the child is skipped because it appeared in a slightly different form (perhaps with a prefix or suffix or imbedded in a compound word, e.g., *unfair, neatly, backbone*). At the intermediate level, children need to become more diligent and sophisticated in examining words. Then (using their sight vocabulary and word attack skills), they should be able to read all the words with which they are familiar, leaving identified as unknown only those words that are really new in meaning to them, words they have never encountered in their previous experience.

Children need a great deal of guidance and practice to enable them to make a good stab at figuring out on their own the meanings of words they have identified as new and are encountering for the first time. The teacher can help them to use various techniques as they read normal reading matter together. But, in order to systematically train children in the use of these techniques, practice in the form of teacher-made exercises which focus on one skill at a time is very helpful. Examples of such exercises follow.

USING CONTEXT CLUES. Leave the unknown word blank, or substitute a nonsense word and ask children to guess what word should really go in there. Then put the original word in the sentence; the chances are that the children have already guessed it, or have provided very useful synonyms for it.

Mary _____ down the street as fast as she could go. (dashed)

Mother took _____ for her headache. (Excedrin)

Father worked so hard, he was *throop.* (exhausted)

For dessert Mother made *shumbol.* (soufflé)

We cleaned and scrubbed the house until it was _____. (immaculate)

"Nobody wants to play with me," he said _____. (forlornly)

In using context clues for guessing, going from the general to the specific is a logical approach:

When Mary tasted the dessert, she was surprised to find it was tart.

a) Tart tells about

Mary
the dessert

b) Tart tells

what color
how many
what taste
how big

c) If Mary was surprised, "tart"
probably means

sweet
sour.

Bob became very excited and shrieked at the boy.

Bob

a) Shrieked tells what the boy did.

b) Shrieking is probably a way of

walking
talking
looking.

loud

c) Shrieking is a soft way of talking.

d) Shrieked means

whispered
screamed.

When they got to the studio, the artist himself opened the door to let them in.

a) Studio tells   <u>where</u>
                     <u>when</u>
                     <u>who.</u>

                              <u>a teacher</u>
b) Studio is a place for   <u>a student</u>
                              <u>an artist.</u>

USING LINGUISTIC CLUES. Although most of these skills will be more fully developed at the advanced level, many intermediate children will have a sufficiently developed linguistic sense to be able to attack new words linguistically if they are guided in how to do this by teacher demonstrations and by teacher-made exercises. They can become sensitive to the clues offered by the construction of the sentence (e.g., parallel constructions, phrases), and can learn to do some word analysis, finding the roots of words and learning some prefixes and suffixes, as well as such form class markers as *ed* and *ing* verb endings, *er* and *ist* noun endings, *ly* adverb endings.

Find a word in the sentence that has the same meaning as the underlined phrase.

Susan's <u>mother and father</u> came to visit, but Mary's parents did not show up.

Jean had to decide what to wear to the party but she just couldn't <u>make up her mind.</u>

<u>At last</u> the great day came, and Jack finally got his driver's permit.

When Mary said she <u>wouldn't go,</u> Joan also refused.

Mary had <u>one or two</u> pencils and several pens.

Mary likes <u>strawberry</u> ice cream best, but her brother prefers chocolate.

Find a word in the underlined word that helps you with the meaning.

John's father is an <u>electrician.</u> He fixes

   chairs   toilets   lights

When the students met with the principal, John was the <u>spokesman</u> for the students. John

   talked   drew pictures   played ball

Alan rested until he <u>regained</u> his strength. Alan became

   stronger   weaker   restless

Sue and Robert met through a <u>matchmaker</u>. A matchmaker

brings people together   works in a cigarette factory

works in a watch factory

A <u>bracelet</u> is jewelry that goes around the wrist.

<u>Braces</u> are wires that go _____ the teeth.

When you <u>embrace</u> someone, you put your arms _____
that person.

USING THE DICTIONARY. Sometimes the sentence offers no
contextual or grammatic clues to help figure out an unknown word,
e.g., The movie was *tedious*. Beyond knowing that *tedious* describes
the movie in some way, its meaning remains obscure. And
sometimes using context clues gives only a vague idea about the
meaning of an unknown word, e.g., John was very *awkward* when he
took his first dancing lesson. When there are no, or inadequate, clues
available, and a precise meaning is needed in order to render the rest
of the reading matter understandable, the dictionary should be used.
In order to know how to use the dictionary proficiently, intermediate children need:

1. to improve their skill in locating words,
2. to acquire a good working knowledge of what a definition is,
   and
3. to improve their awareness of variations in meanings for the
   same word.

The alphabetizing skills of intermediate children should be
extended through practice exercises and through direct experiences
in using functional materials such as telephone directories. In
addition, they should be made aware of the existence and use of
guide words in the dictionary, e.g.,

On which page would you find <u>tedious</u>?   _____

p. 693 has these guide words: tasteful—team

p. 694 has these guide words: teammate—telephone

p. 695 has these guide words: telescope—temporary

On which page would you find:

kiosk

knelt

kiln

kernel

p. 360 has these guide words: keystone—kindly

p. 361 has these guide words: kindness—knead

p. 362 has these guide words: knee—knowing

Defining words is a very highly specialized skill which requires semantic and grammatic awareness. A definition must not only tell what a word means, it must tell this in the same linguistic form as the word itself. Intermediate children will only make a beginning inroad on the complicated task of *giving* definitions. However, they should gain a fairly good *understanding* of definitions as given by others, or specifically, as given in the dictionary. Structured activities can help build up a concept of a definition. For example, in one week's concentrated work on definitions, the teacher presented the class with a different home-made crossword puzzle each day. Each puzzle had been constructed using only one type of definition.

The first puzzle used the class or category as the defining phrase. The page in the dictionary on which each defined word could be found was given. (Almost every entry chosen was illustrated in the dictionary the children were using.)

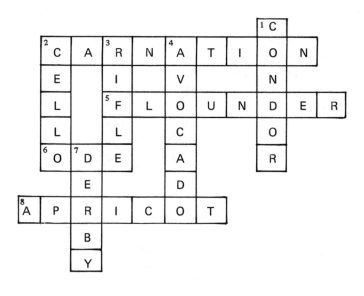

	Across		Down
	2-A kind of flower (p.)		1-A kind of bird (p.)
	5-A kind of fish (p.)		2-A musical instrument (p.)
	6-A kind of poem (p.)		3-A kind of gun (p.)
	8-A summer fruit (p.)		4-A tropical fruit (p.)
			7-A kind of hat (p.)

See Appendix D for illustration of these puzzles.

The second puzzle used synonyms as definitions. In this case, the teacher tried to choose defining words the children would not know (so they would have to consult the dictionary), but familiar words for the answers.

ACROSS	DOWN
1-Penmanship (handwriting)	2-Tidy (neat)
5-Detest (hate)	3-Wealthy (rich)
7-Error (mistake)	4-Examination (test)
8-Shatter (break)	6-Reply (answer)

For the next puzzle, definitions which told the use, purpose or function were used. The page in the dictionary on which each word could be found was given, and usually the dictionary also had a picture.

ACROSS

2-Straps worn over the shoulders to hold up the trousers
        (p.   ) (suspenders)
4-A small, powerful automobile used by the army
        (p.   ) (jeep)
7-A person who makes eyeglasses (p.   ) (optician)
8-A person who spoils other people's fun (p.   ) (killjoy)
9-A long rope used for catching horses and cattle
        (p.   ) (lasso)

DOWN

1-A machine for lifting and moving heavy objects
        (p.   ) (derrick)
3-An instrument used by doctors to listen to the heart and
        lungs (p.   ) (stethoscope)
5-A drug that is very dangerous to life and health
        (p.   ) (poison)
6-A spoon for dipping out liquids (p.   ) (ladle)

The next puzzle concentrated on definitions that described the object, action or idea. The children were told on which page in their dictionary each word could be found.

ACROSS

3-A broad-brimmed hat worn by people in the Southwest,
    Mexico, and Spain (p.   ) (sombrero)
5-A person who has been in the army or navy (p.   )
    (veteran)
7-A small sore on the eyelid (p.   ) (sty)
8-To burn someone or something with hot liquid
    (p.   ) (scald)
9-To run away with a lover (p.   ) (elope)

DOWN

1-Rain gently in very small drops (p.   ) (drizzle)
2-A small, closed place for a public telephone (p.   ) (booth)
3-A long piece of cotton or silk worn as a dress by Hindu
    women (p.   ) (sari)
4-An eyeglass for one eye (p.   ) (monocle)
6-A stop in fighting (p.   ) (truce)

The last puzzle combined all the different types of definitions
used in the previous puzzles.

ACROSS

1-A doctor who treats animals (p.   ) (veterinarian)
5-A long, straight cut (p.   ) (slit)
6-A corpse supposed to come to life at night and suck
    people's blood (p.   ) (vampire)
8-A lasso (p.   ) (lariat)
9-A band of gold and jewels worn around the head
    (p.   ) (tiara)

DOWN

1-A kind of cloth that's thick and rich (p.   ) (velvet)
2-A small child (p.   ) (tot)
3-A pistol that can be fired several times without loading it
    again (p.   ) (revolver)
4-An animal that lives on land and in the water (p.   )
    (amphibian)
7-To go back or to give back (p.   ) (return)

The children analyzed the different ways of defining words and made this chart:

HOW WE TELL WHAT A WORD MEANS

1. Sometimes we give a synonym.
2. Sometimes we tell what kind, or what family—we give the class or group or category that it belongs to.
3. Sometimes we tell what it does or what it's used for.
4. Sometimes we describe it.
5. Sometimes we mix some of 1 - 4.

Other simpler exercises that help give children a sense of what a definition is and of how to use the dictionary to find word meanings follow.

1. Match the phrases to the pictures.

   a) Something worn on the head

   b) A number

   c) A tame animal

   d) A wild animal

   e) Something worn on the feet

2. Complete the sentence:

   A factory is a place where people _____ .
      pray, eat, work, fight.
   January is a _____ .
      season, month, day, winter.

When you are out of breath you _____.
smell, paint, pant, snore.

Someone who is known all over the world is _____.
big, famous, travel, wise.

3. Using the dictionary:

a) On page ___, find the name of an animal.

b) On page ___, find something used to work in a garden.

c) Find a word beginning with the letters pe that means "maybe."

Multiple Meanings. At the primary level, as children were expanding their vocabularies they were usually acquiring the one major meaning for each word they were learning. At the intermediate level, not only do new words keep coming up, but old words with new meanings keep coming up. Sometimes the second and third meanings of a word are vastly different from the original meaning learned, while sometimes there are only shades and nuances of difference which nevertheless affect the meaning of the sentence in important ways. When children consult the dictionary, they will find in many cases that the word they are seeking a meaning for has many different meanings. They have to be able to select the meaning that makes sense in the particular context in which they encountered the word.

The best way I know of to alert children to the prevalence of multiple meanings, and to promote flexibility in shifting from one meaning to another, is through jokes, riddles, and puns. Although these may be hard at first for deaf children (not because deaf children lack humor, but because they are inexperienced at verbal play), once they catch on they love them and retell them gleefully. Here are some old favorites:

(a.)   A: Why are you knitting three socks?

B: Oh, they're for my son. He wrote and told me he grew another foot.

Foot can mean: 1. twelve inches
2. the bottom part of the leg

B's son meant _____ ; B thought he meant _____.

(b).   Customer: Waiter, I'm in a hurry. Will the pancakes be long?
　　　Waiter:　　 Oh, no, sir. They'll be round.

　　　　　　　　Long can tell about:　 1. a shape
　　　　　　　　　　　　　　　　　　 2. an amount of time.

　　　　　　　　The customer meant _____. The waiter thought
　　　　　　　　he meant _____.

(c.)   Customer: Do you serve crabs here?
　　　Waiter:　　 Yes, sir, we serve anyone. Sit right down.

　　　　　　　　A crab can be:　 1. a sourpuss or cranky person
　　　　　　　　　　　　　　　　 2. a kind of seafood

　　　　　　　　The customer meant _____. The waiter meant

　　　　　　　　_____.

(d.)   Riddle:　　 What is the tallest building in New York?
　　　Answer:　　 The Public Library—it has the most stories.

　　　　　　　　Stories means:　 1. floors　　 2. books

　　　　　　　　Which does the library have?

(e.)   Riddle:　　 What did one firecracker say to the other?
　　　Answer:　　 My pop is bigger than your pop.

　　　　　　　　Pop can mean:　 1. noise　　 2. father

　　　　　　　　Which does a firecracker have?

(f.)   Riddle: Why did the lettuce blush?
　　　Answer: It saw the salad dressing.

　　　　　　　　Dressing can mean:　 1. putting clothes on
　　　　　　　　　　　　　　　　　 2. a mixture to put on food

　　　　　　　　Which goes with salad?

(g.)   Riddle: Why was the elephant late in getting on Noah's Ark?

　　　Answer: He was slow in packing his trunk.

　　　　　　　　Trunk can mean:　 1. a large suitcase
　　　　　　　　　　　　　　　　 2. elephant's nose

　　　　　　　　Which was the elephant packing?

Other exercises to provide practice with multiple meanings are:

1. The two pictures show two different meanings for the same word. What is the word?

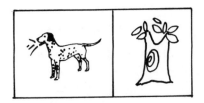

_____ (bark)

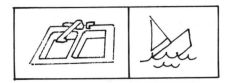

_____ (sink)

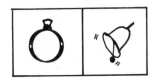

_____ (ring)

_____ (park)

2. The dictionary lists these ten meanings for the word *dash:*

throw	ruin
splash	small amount
rush	a short race
throw and break	a mark used in writing
do quickly	or printing
	energy

Which meaning fits in each of these sentences?

He won the 100-yard dash.

The recipe calls for a dash of pepper.

Mary dashed across the street.

He couldn't fit the last word on the line, so he put a
dash and finished it on the next line.

3. What does *change* mean in each of these sentences?
(Use the dictionary)

I do not have the exact change for the bridge toll.

Let's go by subway for a change.

Susan always changes her mind.

I gave the cashier a dollar and got 10¢ change.

4. What does *strike* mean in each of these sentences?
(Use the dictionary.)

The bus drivers went on strike.

Never strike a child.

Bob got a strike in bowling.

That joke doesn't strike me funny.

He pitched three strikes in a row.

5. The following exercise calls on children to identify unknown
words, guess at their meanings, and then look up their precise
meanings.

Read the story. Then complete the chart.

HE SHOULD HAVE STAYED IN BED.

Don sprinted down the street as fast as he could go. He looked
like a racer in a 100-yard dash. The church bells started to chime and
he counted them as he ran. Nine! He had to hurry.

He was staring straight ahead as he ran and he didn't notice that the streets were deserted. Usually at nine in the morning many people were coming and going. But today there were very few people in the street.

At last he reached the store. He rushed to the door. It was closed! He couldn't believe it. He looked for the sign in the window. It was still there.

```
SALE! SALE! SALE!
COLOR TV SETS
$50 WHILE THEY LAST
ONE DAY ONLY
MONDAY, FEBRUARY 23rd
DOORS OPEN 9:00 A.M.
```

Where were all the people? Why was the store closed, he wondered. He looked at his calendar wrist watch. "Oh, my God!" he groaned. "How could I be such a nincompoop!"

What do you think Don's watch showed?

Pick out all the words you didn't know and list them on the worksheet.

First try to guess what the words mean. Then look them up in the dictionary.

New Word	What do you think it means?	What page did you find it on? Between what guide words?	In this story the word means

Comprehension

At the intermediate level children are introduced to a vast assortment of reading materials and expected to learn to handle these independently. They will need a great deal of careful teacher help and guidance in understanding these materials, especially since deaf children are struggling at the same time to build up their language competencies. At this level, it is extremely helpful to give children an understanding of how various materials differ from each other, as well as of how the purposes in reading may differ. Children will be aided in their comprehension if they do not approach all reading in the same way, but have some idea of the nature of the particular material and of what they should be looking for in reading it. All of us make automatic adjustments in our reading depending upon whether it is a recipe, a novel, a stock market report, a contract, or a newspaper column we are reading. If we spend some time teaching deaf children ways of dealing with different written matter, their comprehension will be aided. Ultimately, they should know more about how information is organized in sources, such as a basal reader, library book, newspaper item or textbook and should be better able to grasp the essence of the material.

Stories. In reading a story the children essentially must be able to visualize the characters and follow the sequence of events as they unfold. The story units become much longer at the intermediate level than at the primary level, and the habit of reading in cumulative thought units must be established. This requires integrating one detail with another; it also means recognizing cause and effect, or anticipating and drawing inferences. Finally, the major idea that ties the whole story together has to be recognized. In building comprehension skills, the teacher has to be very careful about not losing the whole in concentrating on the parts, and vice versa. It's the old problem of seeing both the forest and the trees. In general, children should approach a story with the expectation of finding out who is in it, what happened, how and why it happened. They should also have a personal reaction or judgment, which will in a sense indicate whether they understood the author's intent, and whether the author succeeded in making the desired impact on them. That is, how much they liked the story or found it funny, interesting or informative depends on whether they really understood it, as well as on whether it suited their particular tastes or interests.

The teacher will build up these comprehension skills through direct discussion in individual and group reading sessions. In addition, specific comprehension skills can be developed through workbook and skill-building exercises available commercially or made up by the teacher. Some of the techniques used at the primary level can be adapted for use here by increasing the complexity of the language and the length of the passages. Some examples follow.

1. Match the sentence to the picture. (These sentences may be put in an envelope pasted into a magazine as at the primary level, or the teacher may put the pictures in one envelope and the sentences in another.)

The children are disappointed because of the weather.

This woman cannot make up her mind.

The store must have sent the wrong package to this woman.

The children love the weather.

This man needs some new clothes.

This man is worried that he is late.

2. Find the word that is wrong and change it.

(a.) Many children came to the party. Everybody got a present. The boys got puzzles and the girls got jacks. They were so pleased. When Johnny got home he showed his mother the jacks he got at the party.

(b.) Johnny thought he would have to skip the refreshments because he must not eat anything made with chocolate. They served chocolate cup cakes and vanilla ice cream. For drinks you could choose soda or chocolate milk. So Johnny skipped the cup cakes, but he had milk and ice cream. He was so happy.

(c.) Twice a week Mother bakes pie for dessert. Lorna loves apple pie and Donald loves cherry pie. To be fair to both of them, Mother decided that Tuesdays were for Lorna's favorite and Fridays Donald could have his favorite. Last Tuesday Mother went to the store and bought cherries to bake a pie for that night's dessert.

(d.) Backward Rhyme. This poem is full of contradictions. In each line, find the words that do not go together.

One bright day in the middle of the night,
Two dead boys got up to fight.
Back to back they faced each other,
Drew their swords and shot each other.

A deaf policeman heard the noise,
Came and shot the two dead boys.
If you do not believe this lie is true,
Ask the blind man; he saw it too.

3. Complete the sentences.

(a.) Ted was getting ready to go out. He put on his hat and coat and then he looked out the window. He went and got his umbrella and he put on his rubbers because it was _____ .

(b.) Bobby was helping Mother prepare for his birthday party. He was blowing up balloons to use for decorations. He was very careful with the first balloon and stopped blowing while it was still small. The second balloon was a little bigger, and the third balloon was even bigger. When he got to the fourth balloon he blew and blew until _____ .

(c.) Peter wanted a new bicycle more than anything else in the world. But it cost $80 and he only had $25 saved up. He decided he would try to earn some money. He helped his neighbors wash their cars. He mowed their lawns and ran errands. He put all the money they paid him in his money box. He worked very hard for weeks. One day Peter took all the money out of his savings box and counted it. Then he jumped up and down with joy because _____ .

4. The following stories are accompanied by a battery of tests checking on comprehension of: the main idea, the sequence of events, details, vocabulary, and inferences. Obviously, not every selection read will be treated in this way; the purpose here is chiefly illustrative—to indicate a variety of ways in which various facets of comprehension can be followed up.

THE DONKEY AND THE DOG

A donkey and a dog were traveling with their master. The master stopped to take a nap. The donkey at once began to eat the grass. The dog, who was hungry too, said to the donkey, "Please stoop down so that I may reach the bread that is in the basket on your back."

But the donkey refused, saying, "Wait until our master wakes up. He will feed you."

Just then a hungry wolf came out of the woods. "Help me, help me, or the wolf will surely kill me," cried the donkey.

The dog replied, "Wait until our master wakes up. He will help you."

But, alas, the master didn't awake in time.

a) What happened to the donkey?

b) What lesson did the dog teach the donkey?

☐   Do unto others as you would have them do unto you.

☐   Don't put all your eggs in one basket.

☐   Don't put off till tomorrow what you can do today.

c) Arrange these sentences in the right order: Write the numbers 1 - 7 next to each sentence to tell what happened 1st, 2nd, etc.

☐   The donkey ate some grass.

☐   The wolf ate the donkey.

☐   The master went to sleep.

☐   The donkey would not help the dog.

☐   A wolf came out of the woods.

☐   The dog wanted to eat some bread.

☐   The dog would not help the donkey.

d) Choose the best answer.

(1)   The master stopped because he was

hungry   sleepy   afraid

(2)   The donkey was

hungry   sleepy   tired

(3)   The dog was

hungry   sleepy   tired

(4)   The donkey ate

grass   bread   nothing

(5)   The dog wanted

grass   bread   nothing

(6)   The dog couldn't reach the bread because it was

      in a basket on the ground
      on the donkey's back
      in the master's pocket

(7)   The dog wanted the donkey

      to wake the master
      to give him some grass
      to bend down

(8)   The donkey   helped   the dog.
                didn't help

(9)   The donkey wanted the dog to help him

      get the bread
      wake the master
      fight the wolf

(10)   The dog   helped   the donkey.
            didn't help

e) Is the sentence true or false?

(1)	The donkey was selfish.	T	F
(2)	The dog was kind.	T	F
(3)	The donkey helped the dog.	T	F
(4)	The dog saved the donkey.	T	F
(5)	The wolf killed the donkey.	T	F
(6)	The wolf killed the dog.	T	F
(7)	The master saved the donkey.	T	F
(8)	The master saved the dog.	T	F

f) Answer the questions:

(1)   Why did the master stop?
(2)   What did the donkey eat?
(3)   Why didn't the dog eat?
(4)   What did the dog want the donkey to do?
(5)   Why didn't the donkey help the dog?
(6)   Why didn't the dog help the donkey?

g) What do these words mean?

(1) When you take a *nap* you

        eat   ride   sleep

(2) When you *stoop* you

        bend   jump   stop

(3) *Refuse* means   say yes

                        say no

(4) When you *reply* you

        jump   talk   eat

TOMMY

Tommy is a curly haired little boy who is always getting in trouble. Everybody on his block calls him "the little rascal." His mother, Mrs. White, usually tries to keep an eye on him, but one day she was busy as a bee and couldn't watch him. She had invited lots of people for dinner and had to get ready for them. She woke up at the crack of dawn and baked a chocolate cake. She put the cake on the table to cool. Then she started to clean the house.

While his mother was up in the bedroom, Tommy quietly slipped into the kitchen. His eyes opened wide and his mouth watered when he saw the delicious chocolate cake.

Suddenly Mrs. White heard a THUD! She flew down the steps and ran into the kitchen. There was Tommy, sitting on the floor, with chocolate cake all over him.

Mrs. White groaned; she picked Tommy up and gave him a good spanking.

a) A good title for this story would be:

Busy Mother

A Troublemaker

A Delicious Chocolate Cake

Would you like Tommy for a brother?

If you were Mrs. White, what would you do to Tommy?

What do you think Mrs. White served for dessert?

b) Tell what happened first, second, third, etc.

Mrs. White heard a loud noise   ☐

Tommy went into the kitchen.   ☐

Mrs. White spanked Tommy.   ☐
Mrs. White baked a chocolate cake.   ☐
Mrs. White went up to clean the bedroom.   ☐
Tommy tried to take the cake.   ☐
She put the cake on the kitchen table.   ☐

c) Choose the right answer.

   (1)   How old is Tommy?
               8, 3, 5, it doesn't tell

   (2)   Mrs. White baked a cake
               for a birthday party   for Tommy

               for company

   (3)   The story took place
               on a Saturday   in the summer
               it doesn't tell

   (4)   Mrs. White put the cake on the table because
               there was no room in the refrigerator
               the cake was too hot   the cake was too cool

   (5)   When Tommy saw the cake, he was
               disappointed   happy   angry   worried

   (6)   Mrs. White rushed into the kitchen because
               she smelled the cake burning
               she saw Tommy eating the cake
               she heard a noise

   (7)   What made the loud noise?
               the table broke   the cake fell down

               Tommy broke a dish

   (8)   How did Mrs. White feel?
               angry   pleased   frightened   amused

   (9)   Mrs. White
               was proud of Tommy
               punished Tommy
               forgave Tommy

d) Answer the following questions.

(1)   What is the little boy's name?

(2)   Why does his mother always have to watch him?

(3)   Why couldn't Mrs. White watch Tommy on the day of the story?

(4)   What did she make for dessert?

(5)   Why didn't Mrs. White see Tommy go into the kitchen?

(6)   What happened to the cake?

e) Choose the right answer.

(1)   A little rascal is a child who is

      polite   rude   naughty   sweet

(2)   To keep an eye on somebody means

      to watch   to examine   to ignore

(3)   Mrs. White woke up at the crack of dawn. This means

      she woke up late

      she woke up early

      a noise woke her

      a crack woke her

(4)   When Tommy slipped into the kitchen, he

      fell   tiptoed   whispered

(5)   We groan when we are

      happy   sad   sleepy

(6)   When Mrs. White flew down the stairs, she

      slid down   ran down   fell down   rode down

because she was

      hungry   in a hurry   happy

Directions. Very precise reading of step-by-step details is required in following directions, and often the vocabulary can be difficult or technical. Riddles, directions for cooking, tricks, and games can provide practice in reading without having the tedium kill motivation. This kind of material also shows children for whom stories have no appeal that there are other reading materials that may be of greater interest to them. I have seen deaf adults who were practically illiterate read the sports column in a newspaper as though it were duck soup.

1. Riddles. Usually riddles involve verbal play; but some riddles depend on careful visualizing of details in order to uncover the logical (or illogical) flaw.

    (a) One duck in front of two ducks,
        One duck behind two ducks,
        One duck between two ducks.
        How many ducks all together?
          (Answer: three)

    (b) There are ten brothers in the Jones family. Each brother has a sister. How many children are there in the family?
          (Answer: eleven)

    (c) Ten men were standing under one small umbrella, yet not one of them got wet. How come?
          (Answer: It wasn't raining.)

    (d) Joe was walking along the street one day. His friend stopped him and said, "Say, you're wearing one black sock and one brown sock." Joe replied, "Isn't that funny? I have another pair just like that at home."
        How come Joe has such strange pairs of socks?

2. A Party Game. Have the class read this together and then play it:

This is a simple game, but it is a lot of fun because what you say and what you do don't agree. Here's how to play it:

The first player points to some part of his body and says, "This is my _____." But instead of saying the correct word, he names a different part of the body! For example, he may touch his nose and say, "This is my elbow."

The next player has to touch the part of the body that was named by the player before her, but she has to call it something else. So she touches her elbow but has to call it something else, e.g., she can say, "This is my eyebrow." The next player has to touch his eyebrow, but call it something else.

If you make a mistake, you're out. Try to name as many different parts of the body as you can.

3. A Card Trick. This should be read by the teacher and the children together one step at a time (covering up everything but the sentence being read), and each action carried out as it is read.

For this trick you need to take 13 cards from the deck—Ace through King.

You have to arrange the cards in a special order:

> Five will be the first card and all the other cards will go behind five as follows:
>
> > five, nine, ten, King, Jack, two, four,
> > six, Queen, Ace, seven, eight, three

Hold the cards face down (the five will be at the bottom).
Put the top card on the bottom and say, "A."
Put the next card on the bottom and say, "C."
Put the next card on the bottom and say, "E."
Put the next card on the table. Turn it face up. It is the Ace.
Put the next card on the bottom and say, "T."
Put the next card on the bottom and say, "W."
Put the next card on the bottom and say, "O."
Put the next card on the table. Turn it face up. It is the two.
Continue in the same way. Spell out three, four, five, etc. and put the top card on the bottom as you say each letter. When you finish spelling a number, turn the next card face up. It will be the number you just spelled.

4. Farmyard. This is a funny card game, and should be played by four or five people. (In this case, it is best to have the children read through all the directions first and then go back and reread them, and do what it says, step by step.)

First, each player chooses a farm animal. All the players have to remember everybody's animal.

All the cards in the deck are dealt out to the players. The players do not pick up their cards, but leave them in neat piles face down in front of them.

The first player picks up the top card from his pile and puts it face up in a second pile right next to his closed pile.

The next player does the same thing, and so on. Each player in turn puts the top card from his closed pile face up in a second open pile.

If a player turns up a card that is the same as another player's card, both players must quickly make the sound of the other's animal. For example, suppose you are a cow. You turn over a Jack. Another player who went before you also has a Jack. This player is a pig. You have to try to say "oink oink" before that player says "moo." Whoever makes the sound first, gets the other player's open cards.

The game is over when one player has won all the cards. Or, if you want to put a time limit on the game, the player who has the most cards when the time is up, wins.

5. A recipe for taffy apples.

Wash and dry 12 apples.

Insert a wooden skewer into the stem end of each apple to make a handle.

Place in a saucepan:

1 cup molasses	1 teaspoon vinegar
1 cup sugar	1/3 teaspoon salt
	1/4 cup water

Stir with a spoon to blend the mixture.

Place the saucepan on the stove and boil the syrup mixture. Put a candy thermometer in it. When it registers 270 degrees, remove the syrup from the fire.

Add 2 tablespoons butter, or butter substitute, and stir to blend.

Place the saucepan in a bowl of hot water.

Dip the apples into the hot syrup, making sure to cover the entire surface of each apple.

As you remove an apple from the syrup, twist it to spread the syrup evenly. Place the apples on wax paper to cool.

6. Directions for making a game.

Get three tin cans of about the same size. Put them on the floor, one behind the other, and each about two feet apart.

Now you have to make rings. Get some heavy cardboard and two plastic lids. One lid should be about three inches larger than the cans, and the other lid about two inches larger than the cans. Trace around the larger lid on the cardboard. Then put the smaller lid inside this circle and trace around it. Cut out the ring. Make four rings.

You're now ready to play "Ring-Around-A-Can." Mark off a line about six feet from the nearest can. Each player stands behind the line and throws the four rings, trying to get them around the cans.

You score 5 points for a ring around the nearest can; 10 points for a ring around the middle can; and 15 points for a ring around the farthest can.

The first player to score 50 points is the winner.

Textbooks and Periodicals

The introduction of non-fiction materials marks this level as the beginning of the "reading to learn" period. From my point of view, labeling this kind of reading as reading for information in contrast to the reading of fiction materials for pleasure is unfortunate. Not only does this imply that stories are not informative and mind-stretching, and works of non-fiction not enjoyable, but it lends support to a tendency to approach this kind of reading as a searching out of facts and details. If we can keep in mind in teaching reading that all reading can feed the mind as it nourishes the spirit, and that in all reading the parts become significant as they contribute to a whole concept of one kind or another, then making distinctions between different materials can be safe and helpful.

To some extent, the way we read depends on the nature of the material itself, and to some extent the way we read depends on our particular purpose in reading. There are some times when the same material may be read in different ways. If, for example, you were casually skimming a newspaper item and suddenly came upon the name of a person you know, you'd very likely go back and read the article much more carefully. In teaching children how to deal with textbooks and periodical materials, they should be made aware of the special nature and organization of each type of content material, and of their own purposes in reading them.

Math and Science Materials. These are similar in some ways and, like reading directions, usually call for careful, precise reading with close attention to the details. However, noting details is not enough; it is the quality of thinking in handling the details that makes for successful problem-solving in the sciences and social sciences. Deaf children often pick out the details and use whatever mathematical or scientific processes they have mastered to juggle them to a solution. An organized approach that takes into account the nature of the material would be more effective. The procedure suggested here might be helpful:

a) Identify what is given or known.

b) Identify what question or problem is posed, what is unknown.

c) Hypothesize an answer (in math, will the answer be greater or less than the given numbers; in science, what effect can be anticipated?).

d) Execute your plan of action, carefully using known mechanics.

e) Check the reasonableness of the answer. This means checking to see that no mechanical errors were made, but it also means using plain logic to find possible errors in reasoning even if the mechanics were flawless. For example, suppose in solving a math problem you had an answer that was not consistent with your experience (e.g., a price that seemed wrong); you might check your approach rather than just your computations.

This desirable approach will be developed gradually with the use of actual curricular materials. In addition, practice exercises can focus on one or more aspects of this process.

1. Indicate whether each fact is necessary or unnecessary, and whether enough information has been given.

   a) Susan is five years older than Mary. Mary's birthday is on March 5. How old will she be?

   b) There are four boys and three girls in the Book Club. Each boy took two books out of the library. Each girl took out three books. How many books did they all take?

   c) Mr. Jones bought a dozen pencils for 48¢. He bought two pens for 24¢. How much did each pencil cost?

2. Choose the answer you think is most likely.

   a) John is older than Mary, but younger than Tim. Tim is 11.
      (1) Mary is less than 11.
      (2) Mary is more than 11.

   b) John saved 50¢ a week. After five weeks, he found that he had enough to buy a bat, but not enough for the catcher's glove he wanted.
      (1) The glove cost less than $2.50.
      (2) The glove cost more than $2.50.

3. Air Pressure

   If you ever asked someone why an airplane can fly you were probably told, "air pressure." You probably do not really understand what this means. It is hard to believe that the invisible air that is all around us is so strong that it can help keep a plane in the air. Air has weight, and it presses strongly against anything that gets in its way. Try these experiments and see what they show you about air pressure.

a) Fill a glass with water right up to the top. Cover the glass with a square piece of cardboard. Now quickly turn the glass upside down.

   Take the hand that was holding the cardboard away. Do you think the cardboard will fall and the water will spill out? It won't.

   Why?

b) Put some water in a glass. Sip some of the water into a straw. While the straw is filled with water take it out of the water and quickly put your finger over the top of the straw.

   Will the water fall back into the glass? Why?

   Now remove your finger from the top of the straw. Will the water fall back into the glass now? Why?

c) Get two apples. Get two pieces of string, each one about two feet long. Tie one end of each string around the stem of each apple.

   Tie the other ends of the string around a towel rack or bar so that the apples are hanging down about an inch apart.

   Now blow hard between the two apples.

   Will they blow apart or come together and bump? Why?

Social Studies Materials. Whether it is a book, a magazine or newspaper article, a reference or text book, the content is generally arranged in some chronological or logical order. To understand the material, the reader has to grasp the main or overall idea, and perceive how the details relate to, build up and support the main ideas. For deaf children, this process is interfered with and made more complicated by language complexities and, sometimes, by an insufficient background of experience with which to understand the concepts presented. It is important to minimize these stumbling blocks in order to free the children to concentrate on the skill of organizing ideas as they read. It is also helpful if some of the component skills are developed separately through special exercises, so that children may later integrate these skills in using regular curricular materials. Examples follow:

a) Select the key sentence in the paragraph.

   Very, very early in man's history, man lived outdoors. When the weather was fine, there was no problem, but when the rains and storms came man had no protection. And when enemies, human or animal, attacked, man was at their mercy. Soon man discovered that he could hide in caves. And from then on began the building of houses. Today there are houses of every size, shape, material. Whether they are big or small, round or square, made of wood, stone, grass or ice, the main purpose of any house is to provide shelter to those who live in it.

b) Putting a list of topics in order

c) Matching headings with paragraphs

d) Selecting the chief idea and the subordinate ideas in a paragraph

For many years, thousands of people died of Yellow Jack each year. This was the name given to the dread disease of yellow fever. In 1900, the American army was in Cuba fighting with the Cubans against the Spanish. More soldiers died of Yellow Jack than were killed in the war.

No one knew what caused this terrible sickness. Most doctors and scientists thought it was spread by a germ. But one man, Dr. Carlos Finlay, said that yellow fever was caused by a certain mosquito.

The U.S. Army sent a doctor, Major Walter Reed, to Cuba to find out what could be done about Yellow Jack. He saw that some people got the disease, and other people who lived in the same house did not.

Dr. Reed decided to do an experiment to see whether yellow fever was caused by a germ or by a mosquito. He had two little houses built outside of town. They had screens on all the doors and windows. In one house he put the dirty linens and pajamas of men who had yellow fever. The other house was spotlessly clean and free of all germs, but it had fifteen yellow fever mosquitoes.

Some men stayed in each house for about three weeks. Then they came out. The men in the house with germs but no mosquitoes were all right. But the men in the clean house with mosquitoes got yellow fever. This proved that the cause was the mosquito.

Now, at last, people knew what to do to stop the disease. They wiped out the mosquitoes that were in the swamps. Today you almost never hear of any cases of yellow fever.

Next to each topic, write a number from 1 to 6 to tell which paragraph the topic belongs with. Then write <u>M</u> if you think it is the main idea of the paragraph, or <u>H</u> if it is a helping detail.

Is it a germ or a mosquito?

Cause *is* the mosquito

Walter Reed investigates

More soldiers killed by fever than by guns

Results of the experiment

Drain swamps, kill mosquitoes

Experiment to pin down cause

Yellow fever—a killing disease

Yellow fever can be cured

Cause unknown

Germs do not attack all in one house

House with germs vs. house with mosquitoes

e) Recognizing the main ideas and selecting the facts and details presented in support of the main ideas.

Wyoming is the land of cowboys and bucking horses. Near Cheyenne, Wyoming, the land usually does not get much rain. Very little of the land near Cheyenne, therefore, is farmed. Except for some small gardens near the homes and some fields near streams, the land is all in grass.

The people who live around Cheyenne raise cattle and sheep. The ranches are very large. With so little rain, the grass grows slowly and it takes a large field of grass to feed a few cattle.

There are eight states in the United States with more land than Wyoming, but only two states have fewer people. Not many people live in Wyoming. The land cannot be irrigated and almost nothing grows except a little grass and sage brush. The high Rocky Mountains cover much of western Wyoming. It is hard to earn a living from the land.

From the list of sentences below, pick out the three main ideas presented in these paragraphs. Label them I, II, III.

Then, under each main idea, copy the sentence that tells why.

The grass grows slowly.

It's hard to make a living.

The ranches in Wyoming have to be large.

Wyoming is a large state with a small population.

It is easier to raise cattle and sheep than farm products.

A lot of grass feeds only a few cattle.

f) The selections that follow are based on newspaper articles, one from *My Weekly Reader,* and one from *The News.* The questions illustrate the various ways children may be guided in organizing information read.

LET'S PLAY A GAME

In the city of Rome, Italy, some faded lines are scratched on an old stone street. They were made about 1,900 years ago. What are they? They are markings for a hopscotch game! Long, long ago children played this game. And today it is still played by boys and girls all over the world. It is played in many different ways and has many different names.

In France, this game is called La Marelle. In Scotland, children call it Teevers. In Russia, the hopscotch game is called Gareeka.

Some children draw squares for the game. Others use snail shapes or triangles. In many games, the children hop. Sometimes they leap or jump—frontwards, backwards or sideways. Sometimes children jump with eyes closed. Boys and girls in Burma sit down on their heels and jump while squatting.

First expose the story briefly and ask the children to read it quickly for the main idea:

The story tells about

a) a game that was played a long time ago

b) a game that children play all over the world

c) a game that children play in Europe

d) how children are different

Then once again expose the story briefly and have the children skim it to find this one fact:

What is hopscotch called in Scotland?

Then allow children to reread it at their normal pace, telling them to remember as many facts as they can so they can answer these questions:

a) How old is hopscotch?

b) Who plays it?

c) Where is it played?

d) Does everyone call it hopscotch?

e) Does everyone play it the same way?

f) Show me how they play it in Burma.

OUTLINING

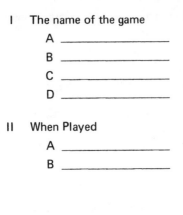

I   The name of the game

    A _____

    B _____

    C _____

    D _____

II   When Played

    A _____

    B _____

III   _____

    A   All over the world

    B   Outdoors, on the sidewalk

IV   How played

    A _____

      1 _____

      2 _____

      3 _____

    B _____

      1 _____

      2 _____

      3 _____

TWO ROCK COLLECTORS
EXPLORE A NEW FIELD

By Alton Slagle
Staff Correspondent of The News

Houston, Tex., July 20—Pick up a rock, put it in your pocket. Sounds simple. Every boy does it. Except in this case the rock is on the moon—and the pocket is in a pressurized spacesuit.

That's one of the many jobs Neil Armstrong and Buzz Aldrin had on the moon. That rock in the pocket was about the first item of business when Armstrong stepped out of Eagle at 10:56 tonight. It was the first of up to 100 pounds of lunar material the astronauts went up to collect and bring back to earth.

Here, after a period of quarantine, the material will be studied, re-studied and studied again to glean knowledge from every precious atom.

That first rock was gathered quickly, just in case, for any reason, the spacemen had to get back into Eagle and blast away immediate-ly. They wanted at least one lunar sample to bring home. And they got it.

With a scoop on an extension handle, Armstrong gathered the first soil ever obtained from the moon. He placed it in a Teflon bag and stuffed it in his left-hand pocket, a difficult job because he could not see the pocket of the inflated suit.

"Is my pocket open, Buzz?" he asked the Eagle's pilot.
"Yes, it is," Aldrin answered.
"Is it in the pocket?"
"Yeah, push down. No, it's not all the way down. Push it."
"Okay, the sample is in the pocket," Armstrong said.

Main Idea (title; 1st paragraph)

What is special about these rock collectors?

     1 –

     2 –

Getting the facts

2nd paragraph	What did the astronauts do first when they stepped out on the moon? What will they bring back to earth?
3rd paragraph	What will be done with the things they bring back from the moon at first? then?
4th paragraph	Why was the first rock collected fast? (What might make the astronauts leave right away? Not in the story—think for yourself.)
	How did Armstrong pick up the first rock? What did he do with the first rock? How did Aldrin help him?

Organizing the facts

    I   What did the astronauts collect on the moon?

   II   How did they collect it?

 III   Why?

Skimming Most of the time when children are reading for information they do need to read carefully and organize what they are reading. However, there are times when just skimming material is all that is necessary. For example, if you want to look through something quickly to see if it is what you want or need; when you are choosing a book for your own recreational reading; or when you are looking up something in a book, it is better to skim than to read carefully. When children are re-reading or studying something they have already discussed, they should be taught to skim. In other words, children should learn to vary their approach according to the material as well as according to their own purpose in reading.

A helpful device to demonstrate different reading techniques is to have children read a paragraph first for one purpose and then reread the paragraph for another purpose. For example, ask the pupils to skim this paragraph rapidly, ignoring details.

> NY Times, July 14, Bridgeport, Conn. The engineer was killed and 24 persons were injured today when the Federal, crack New Haven Railroad train, jumped the rails on a sharp curve just south of the Bridgeport station.

After a brief exposure, cover the paragraph and ask the pupils to select the phrase which best tells what the item was about:

A plane accident.

An automobile accident.

A train accident.

A train robbery.

Now ask pupils to reread the paragraph; this time they are to pay careful attention to details. Then ask the following questions:

Comprehension of detail:

Where did the accident take place?

How many people were killed?

How many people were hurt?

What was the name of the train?

Main idea:

How did the accident happen?

Inferences:

How many people were on the train?

less than 24   24   25   at least 25

What caused the accident?

The engineer fell asleep.

The train was going too fast.

The story doesn't say.

The rails were slippery.

Assigning just one question about a selection encourages children to wade through difficult language in order to get the main idea or to find a specific fact. For example, present the following selection and ask only: What change did Clara Barton make in the Red Cross?

> Clara Barton convinced the United States Government that it should join the International Red Cross. Twenty-two nations were already giving money and supplies to this organization to help soldiers in wartime.

But Clara Barton added another idea to this great Red Cross plan. It was called the American Amendment.

"There are many other calamities that befall mankind," she said, "earthquakes, floods, forest fires, epidemics, tornadoes. These disasters strike suddenly, killing and wounding many, leaving others homeless and starving. The Red Cross should stretch out a hand of help to all such victims, no matter where such disasters befall."

Today, the International Red Cross brings succor to millions of people all over the world.

Book Reports

The only true test of the effectiveness of the reading program is the extent to which the skills taught are used by the children in their independent reading. Faced with enormous obstacles in the form of new and abstract vocabulary, sentence structure and concepts, intermediate children can easily become discouraged and regard reading as a chore rather than a pleasure. The reading program would fail to achieve its purpose if children read only when they had to and rarely because they just wanted to. Recreational reading activities can do much to revive children's self-confidence and enthusiasm.

To help children develop independence in selecting materials to suit their own interests, they should be exposed to a wide variety of materials. Often an intense interest enables children to successfully read some difficult reading materials when these same children are experiencing failure in basal readers, skill builders, and reading tests. Teachers and librarians should encourage children to explore widely the riches available through reading. Book displays, inviting authors, trips to the local library can demonstrate to children that reading is more than plowing through a series of skill-building exercises. Biographies, how-to books, mysteries, science books, magazines, comics, all should be available. Teachers and librarians should act as guides in helping the children find materials they might enjoy and in assisting them with comprehension when they want such help. Teachers and librarians should show an active interest in children's recreational reading, but should not exhibit anxiety about their comprehension. Children should be allowed to take out whatever they are interested in, regardless of whether it seems to the adult to be too easy or too hard for them.

The amount of checking on children's free choice reading should be kept to a minimum. Sometimes the teacher or librarian should do no more than ask whether the child enjoyed the book. Sometimes a one-to-one discussion of the book will enhance the child's enjoyment (especially if the teacher or librarian happens to really like the book the child chose). Sometimes group sessions in which children share their reactions to the books they read can be profitable. Often children will look at the sign-out list in the back of their library book and go talk to another child who had the book before.

Book reporting can be profitable if it does not become an onerous activity. Children should not have to do a book report on every book they read. If book reporting is regarded more as a way a child can share a book with others than as a way of checking on the child's comprehension, it can be very useful. Doing an informative, interesting book report is a difficult job, and this skill has to be developed gradually. At the beginning, just the barest factual information is given. Little by little children may learn to tell what a book was like and whether or why they liked or didn't like it.

For starters, teachers can provide an outline or check list that children may use if they want to.

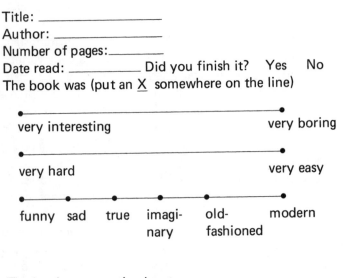

Title: _____

Author: _____

Number of pages:_____

Date read: _____ Did you finish it?   Yes   No

The book was (put an <u>X</u> somewhere on the line)

•————————————————•
very interesting   very boring

•————————————————•
very hard   very easy

•———•———•———•———•———•
funny   sad   true   imagi-   old-   modern
                      nary   fashioned

The book was mostly about

people   _____
animals   _____
sports   _____
history   _____
science   _____

The most difficult part of book reporting is telling something about the book and about your reaction to it, or its impact on you. Learning to tell enough to give an idea of the content without giving away the whole story is difficult. It involves the ability to summarize or retell in your own words, to generalize and not get bogged down in details, and to select specific illustrative points. The teacher will have to work on these skills separately, giving children practice in reading short paragraphs and then paraphrasing them, picking out highlights or key incidents in a selection, telling what they liked best or least about a character or book. These skills can be developed at a simple level with intermediate children and concentrated on in depth later on. The following book reports were written by the same pupil three years apart.

Marie   Dec. 5, 1957
Miss Schaffer   Middle school III

"The Very Little Girl"

What an adorable book I read! I read "The Very Little Girl." The author of my book is Phyllis Krasilovsky. The illustrator is Ninon.

"The Very Little Girl" is about a little girl who was VERY, VERY, VERY, very little and who grew bigger, bigger, bigger and BIGGER. I had a wonderful time reading it.

Wilder, Laura Ingalls
These Happy Golden Years
Harper & Brothers, 1953
Garth Williams
Fiction

This story is about a young pretty lady, Laura and her husband.

Laura got a job teaching children in a brand new schoolhouse. And Laura and Almanzo became engaged. In the spring they were married and went to live in a little grey house in the west. Laura explored the rooms in the house and her heart was full of happiness. "It is a wonderful night," Almanzo said. "It is a beautiful world," said Laura.

Language Obstacles

I have indicated that I believe that the greatest gap between deaf children's actual language level and the language they encounter in reading occurs at the intermediate level. At the primary level, books and other materials were relatively simple and concrete, and at the advanced level, although the vocabulary and grammar are complicated beyond deaf children's actual level, presumably the children will have developed the minimal linguistic skill required to deal with this. The burden on children and teachers in the intermediate school is great and necessitates resourcefulness and flexibility. The teacher must somehow promote the children's reading and language skills at the same time, but not necessarily through the same materials, or in the same activity.

If, by reading skill, we refer to the children's ability to comprehend written material independently, this is best promoted through material with known language. This means that to some extent the material will be teacher-made (original writings, or rewrites of commercial material); or, insofar as is possible, the language of normal material will have been pretaught. Then the children who have progressed satisfactorily in reading should be able to handle such selections.

For example, you have spent some time teaching your children how to select the main idea of a paragraph. Now you would like to check to see if they have mastered this particular reading skill. If you give them a paragraph which has no language complications, they should be able to select the main idea. If they can't, they need more work on this skill. If, however, the paragraph includes unknown words or new constructions which interfere with comprehension, the children may not be able to pick out the main idea. But the failure in this instance may not be due to faulty reading techniques. They do not necessarily need more practice in choosing the main idea. They do, however, need to be taught the language forms they lack. To some extent, as has been indicated, intermediate children can be taught to make a stab at figuring out new language on their own, as difficult as this may be. To the degree that they can do this, they are actually learning new language through reading.

In addition, the teacher will use reading to teach language. Sometimes this is done by incorporating the new language into other class activities in advance of the reading. (For example, teachers can watch to see that the language they themselves use is not always simple, concrete, literal. Incorporating colloquial, interesting expressions, [e.g., "believe it or not," "little did he know," "much to my surprise"] into their conversation with children is good preparation for reading.) Sometimes it is done by explaining the new language as it comes up during the reading. And sometimes it is done by creating exercises to teach specific linguistic constructions.

1. Modified nouns. Draw the picture.

There are four daughters in the McCormick family. *All the girls* have brown hair. *One of the girls* wears eye glasses. *Each girl* is wearing a sweater that matches the color of her eyes. *All except one* have blue eyes.

2. Subject vs. object. Which two sentences are the same?

(a.) John got a letter from his mother.
John wrote a letter to his mother.
John's mother wrote him a letter.

(b.) The mother showed the dog to the baby.
The baby was shown the dog.
The dog was shown the baby.

(c.) The teacher got an apple from the child.
The child got an apple from the teacher.
The teacher gave the child an apple.

3. Inverted sentences. Rewrite the sentence, putting the subject first.

Behind the donkey were ten-year-old Zariefie and her mother.
Clippity-clop over the pavement went the horse's hooves.

4. Passive voice. Change the sentence so that it tells who did the action first.

(a.)   The boy was hit by a car.
(b.)   The old man was helped across the street by a young boy.
(c.)   Occasionally the song was interrupted by the long-drawn howls of wolves.

5. Indefinite pronouns. Draw a line under the words the pronoun refers to.

(a.)   John came late, but Mary didn't mind. <u>What</u> made Mary mad was the way he was dressed.
(b.)   <u>It</u> made Mother sad to hear the boys complain.
(c.)   Tom was surprised to learn his father had served in the war. He didn't know <u>that.</u>
(d.)   When he got to the place he had heard so much about, he didn't recognize <u>it.</u>

6. Modifying phrases and clauses.

(a.)   Make two sentences out of each sentence.
Before he watched television, he finished his homework.
My sister who lives in California is coming to visit us next week.
The man in the blue suit was here yesterday.

(b.)   Which sentences agree with the first sentence?

The boy who hit the baby ran away.

The boy ran away.	Yes	No
The baby ran away.	Yes	No
The baby hit the boy.	Yes	No
The boy hit the baby.	Yes	No

The candy in the bag was hard.

The bag was hard.	Yes	No
The candy was hard.	Yes	No
The candy was in a hard bag.	Yes	No
The hard candy was in a bag.	Yes	No

7. Linguistic constraints. Which word could come next?

He was surprised to	a	see	my	some
Wouldn't you like	pretty	go	to	with
Would you like	take	a	new	dress
She was sure that	see	it	is	went
That's a very	go	for	nice	soon
That's a very pretty	make	for	not	little

8. Question forms.

Deaf children need a great deal of practice before they really understand what specifically is being asked in different question forms. It is helpful to concentrate on drill in one form at a time, in sequence, before mixing all the different question forms in checking comprehension.

a) Who, what, when, where, what color, how many, how often, how long

Questions calling for specific details may be answered in a word or a phrase instead of in a whole sentence to give children a feel for the question word itself. Thus, start with Who questions only, without a written text, drawing only on information children can see or know already. For example:

Who is wearing a red sweater?
Who has a sister named Joan?
Who lives in an igloo?

Then present a written sentence or paragraph with written Who questions only.

Everybody exchanged presents for Christmas. Joanne gave Maria a pen. Sara got a bracelet from Peter. Peter gave Joanne a baseball. Maria gave a game to Peter and a puzzle to Sara. Sara gave Joanne a jump rope and Maria a book.

Who got a puzzle?

Who got a baseball?

Who gave Maria a book?

Who gave Sara a bracelet?

Follow the same procedure for each of the other question forms, first asking questions without a text, next with a text. Then all the questions may be used together.

Two of Robert's cousins came to visit him at school yesterday.

Who visited Robert?

How many people visited Robert?

When did Robert's cousins come?

Where did Robert's cousins come?

b) Questions that call for Yes or No answers. These should be taken up one group at a time until the children get quite used to them. Then they may be mixed. Thus, proceed from Do, Does, Did; to Is, Are, Was, Were; to Will, Can. The written questions can be presented without a text first and then with a given text.

Do, Does, Did questions without a text:

Does this month have 31 days?

Does a chicken have four legs?

Does the sun rise in the west?

Do you have any sisters?

Do four and one make five?

Do cows give eggs?

Did it rain yesterday?

Did you watch TV yesterday?

Did John come to school today?

Do, Does, Did questions based on a text:

Every Sunday morning Mr. and Mrs. Bright go to church. Their son, Peter, and their daughter, Carol, go every other week, because while one goes to church the other stays home to watch the baby. Last Sunday it was Carol's turn to go to church. She was so happy because she loves to wear her best clothes to church.

Does Mr. Bright go to church every week?

Does Carol go every week?

Does Carol like to go to church?

Do all the Bright children go to church?

Do Mr. & Mrs. Bright take their baby to church?

Do Peter and Carol go very week?

Did Peter go to church last week?

Did Carol go to church last week?

Did Carol watch the baby last week?

To Be questions without a text:

Is fourteen an even number?

Are you going to the movies today?

Was anybody absent yesterday?

Were you ever bitten by a dog?

To Be questions based on a text:

Ralph has two brothers and a sister. His brother, Chuck, is younger than Ralph. His brother, Martin, who is older than Ralph was 15 on his last birthday. His sister, Flora, is the oldest child in the family.

Is Chuck less than 15 years old?

Is Martin older than Chuck?

Are all the boys younger than Flora?

Are there four children in the family?

Was Ralph the last child in the family?

Were all the boys born after Flora?

Were any of the children twins?

Mixed Yes—No questions without a text:

Do September and June have the same number of days?

Is an apple a vegetable?

Did the 13th fall on a Friday this month?

Can a woman be the President of the U.S.?

Mixed Yes—No questions based on a text.

Mrs. White took her daughters, Mary and Ruth, shopping. They bought the same dresses, but Mary's was size seven, and Ruth's was size nine.

Are Mary and Ruth sisters?

Do Mary and Ruth wear the same size?

Is Mary bigger than Ruth?

c) Questions of comparison or choice. Children need practice in visualizing what is asked and in understanding that the answer is one of those given. Again, one form should be practiced at a time, without, and then with, a given text, before all forms are mixed.

Without a text:

Which is bigger, a dog or a horse?

Do you want chocolate or vanilla ice cream?

Is Ruth coming today or tomorrow?

Based on a text:

Mark and Mitchell are twins, but they are very different. Mark is quiet and Mitchell is very active. Usually, after supper Mark sits down and reads a book, and Mitchell goes out to play ball. Mark studies a lot and Mitchell never does his homework. Mitchell is on the basketball team and is very popular with the girls.

Who gets better marks, Mark or Mitchell?

Does Mark prefer to work or to play?

Which does Mitchell like better, books or sports?

Would you find Mark in the library or in the gym?

Is Mark alone or with other kids most of the time?

d) How and why questions require a great deal of practice. Children should be helped to distinguish between prepositional phrases that tell where or when, and those that tell how or why, e.g.,

She showed her embarrassment *by lowering her head* as she walked by *the judges' row.*

She wanted to go *to church to see the new minister.*

Most of the skills introduced at the intermediate level will continue to be worked on all through the children's school careers. Successful mastery of intermediate skills is necessary before complete literacy and mature reading can be attained.

DEVELOPMENTAL ACTIVITIES:

6. Advanced

Presumably, basic skills, attitudes, and habits have already been established, and for children ready for this level of work, mature, independent, critical reading will be developed. Deaf children generally enter this level at the age of about 12, and spend about four years here before going on to high school, vocational or trade schools, or jobs. They should complete the work of the 5th to 8th grades to become fully literate. In some schools for the deaf, the advanced level will include high school as well as junior high school work, thus going beyond the 8th grade.

In most schools, the work at this level is departmentalized, meaning that pupils rotate from one teacher to another for the various subjects. Thus, developmental skills in reading are taught not only by the reading teacher during the period specifically allotted, but by all teachers, all day long. In fact, reading becomes the chief avenue for learning. In addition to teaching the special skills and knowledges indigenous to the various curricular areas, each teacher in the rotating department is also teaching reading and language. There should be regular and frequent contact among the various teachers in order to integrate the program and guarantee that skills taught in one area are carried over to other areas. All teachers should become familiar with the specific aims and skills in reading so that they may use their own activities to promote reading skills as well as subject matter skills, and so that they may constantly hold students responsible for using the best reading skills and habits of which they are capable.

It is at the advanced level that you will probably find the greatest individual variations in reading achievement between children within the same age group. The spreads in achievement are enormous, and the gaps between interest and ability are, for some children, devastating. Since reading is a language-based activity, the differences in reading achievement are largely due to differences in linguistic development. The reading program at this level has to be adjusted to meet the very different needs and abilities of various groups of children.

Aims

Those deaf children whose progress has been good have probably acquired by now the minimal skills in language necessary for success in reading. These children are ready for the advanced reading program, and they often make even greater strides in reading at this level than ever before. For these children, the broad aim of the program is to build literal and inferential skills in comprehension that will make reading a permanent source of individual growth and learning. Specifically, these skills involve:

1. Improved comprehension—independently grasping main ideas as well as facts and details; using logic and reason to interrelate facts and details and to draw inferences

2. Reading critically—evaluating what is read, developing personal tastes in reading, judging the usefulness of material according to its own merits and its personal appeal or importance

3. Becoming familiar with a wide range of works of literature

4. Acquiring a working knowledge of reference materials

5. Analyzing vocabulary and language in order to independently learn new language through reading.

Then there will be those children who enter the advanced level still lacking really functional linguistic skills. These may be children with additional handicaps, over and above deafness, that disrupt their ability to learn. Or they may be children with no other known or diagnosed disability, who may do well in non-language-based areas, but to whom somehow or other language remains largely meaningless and impenetrable. It would be unrealistic to require these children to pursue the usual advanced reading program. However, it would be doing them a disservice not to provide them with minimal, basic survival skills in reading. For these children, the minimum aim is the mastery of the functional reading skills necessary for the pursuit of their ordinary life activities. And over and above that, they should acquire the habit of reading to meet their special individual interests and desires (whether it is the sports column of a newspaper, captioned TV or films, comics, or a how-to book of some kind). The teachers can be selective in skimming off parts of the regular program that might be appropriate for these children.

There will generally be still another group somewhere in between the verbal and non-verbal ends of the advanced spectrum. These are children whose linguistic progress has been slow up until the advanced level, but who, somehow or other, through motivation or maturation, now have begun to show greater potential for linguistic growth. With these children the reading program needs to be flexible enough to fill in gaps that were left in earlier skills, while taking into account their newly developing maturity in interest and application. These children will continue to work on intermediate skills, and at the same time they will be exposed to some of the materials and activities in the advanced developmental program.

The teacher at the advanced level has to be a magician and a juggler. The goals, materials, and activities have to be chosen and organized so as to meet individual needs, actual interests, and considerably widespread abilities. This means differentiating the program in many ways. It may sometimes mean using some materials with only some children and not with others; it may sometimes mean using the same materials with all children but at different times and in different ways; it may mean using the same material in the same way with all children at the same time, carefully observing and recording what different children get out of it, and following up with reinforcing activities as needed.

As usual, with *all* students, a wide variety of materials will be used, and particular skills will be taught both through the regular use of normal materials, and by isolating specific skills and providing drill through teacher-made exercises and materials.

Functional Reading

Reading as a means to some other end is a very important part of every person's reading repertoire. It is the core of the reading program for the non-verbal advanced student. Even in the present day and age, with its massive exploitation of the visual media, survival often depends on the ability to interpret the written word. Reading traffic signs, labels on foods and medication, forms·and applications and directions of all kinds is necessary and unavoidable. All advanced students should develop efficiency in reading such materials, and children with the lowest linguistic and reading achievement levels should have a carefully selected and organized program through which they can acquire these basic skills. This will require active participation and cooperation between all the subject matter teachers and the language arts teachers. Certain areas may be covered by the math teacher, others by the social studies teacher, etc. The overall program, however, should take into account and anticipate the children's present and future real life needs and interests.

As activities in each of the following areas are planned, functional reading materials will be introduced and the necessary language and reading skills will be taught.

Jobs—To become familiar with the names of various occupations, and with the qualifications, duties and responsibilities, wage structure, and special benefits of each, children may interview people (school personnel, parents, volunteers, community members); or they may make trips to offices, shops, factories; or see films or filmstrips; or look through books. They will learn how to interpret help wanted ads; how to fill out applications; how to complete various government and union forms. Through discussion, role play, and specially prepared reading materials, they will explore issues such as behavior on a job, training for advancement, handling emergencies, communication problems, etc.

Health and safety—Reading becomes an important survival skill in establishing minimal standards for physical and mental safety and comfort. (For example, in following a doctor's directions, the difference between two pills every three hours and three pills every two hours can be crucial.) Activities should be planned that require interpreting and evaluating resources such as the following: labels and directions on containers of food, cosmetics, drugs, medication; consulting first aid books, height and weight charts, calorie and diet books, recipes, etc.

Personal management—To become independent requires mastering basic reading skills. Handling your own finances involves you with various budgeting, banking, and tax forms. Shopping for food, clothing, shelter, or almost any other supplies and equipment involves reading labels, ads, directions for care and repair, etc. Even if you are deaf and cannot use the phone, the yellow pages can be useful. Knowing how to consult consumers' guides frees you from dependence on high-pressure salespeople.

Social and intellectual life—Having interests and hobbies, even passive ones such as watching TV, involves you with reading. The reading program should build such varied skills as: consulting the TV guide, reading a sports column, following directions for a game, hobby, or craft, interpreting travel folders, timetables, movie reviews, newspaper headlines and captions, current events, etc.

Using Reference Materials

Not all the children in the advanced department will need to be exposed to the full array of skills needed to use all the various reference materials. Those children who are doing very well academically and who will probably continue their formal education beyond the junior high school and high school levels, will benefit from structured sequences of activities designed to develop the ability to work independently in seeking information and in studying. This kind of work, begun here, will be developed gradually throughout the children's academic experience.

Other children will benefit from less detailed work that will nevertheless familiarize them with some of the reference sources available to them and teach them a little bit about how to use these materials when needed. There will always be occasions when they will need or want some piece of information (What's a good portable color TV? Who won the World Series in 1972? What's the weather like in Los Angeles in February? Where does natural gas come from?) To be able to satisfy your own curiosity or needs rather than being dependent on others builds self-esteem. Children at this level should be encouraged to build their own small reference shelf stocked with a dictionary, an atlas, and an almanac, plus whatever other sources may become interesting and meaningful to them. Many youngsters love looking through the Guinness Book of Records, and other reference materials (pictorial biographies and histories) just for fun as well as for specific information.

To use reference sources effectively, many skills are involved. All children at the advanced level should be exposed to activities that will build some of these skills, and some children should have more intensive work and experience with the gamut of study skills:

1. Defining your topic

2. Selecting appropriate reference materials
3. Locating the desired information in the chosen materials
4. Reading, understanding, organizing the information found
5. Evaluating the adequacy of the information found
6. Remembering and using the information

Steps in Using   Usually, the reason for consulting a reference source is to find some needed information—something you want or need to know, information that will settle an argument, or something someone else has assigned you to look up.

You have to be able to identify the topic you should be looking under. For example, suppose you want to know from which country the United States imports the most coffee. Would you look under *coffee, imports, the United States, agriculture, food, drinks?* Children need practice choosing appropriate topic headings for the information they are seeking. They also need to know how to use the card file in the library to find which sources might have information on their chosen topic. For example, if they wanted to know the origin of their own names, they would have to know to look in the card file under *names, language, word origins.*

There are a great many different sources—encyclopedias, almanacs, atlases, *Who's Who,* guidebooks, quotations, and many works of non-fiction from textbooks to biographies to works in science, history, etc. To know where the particular information you want is best found you have to be familiar to some extent with these different sources, know what distinguishes one from another, and what kind of information you can expect to find in each.

After you have chosen the particular source you need for your topic, you have to know how to use it to look up the particular information you want. This involves knowing how the information is organized and presented in the various sources—alphabetically, by topic, chronologically. To find the information on that topic in the reference source you have chosen, you also need to know how to use specific reference aids such as: an index, table of contents, headings, guide words, cross references, and, often, special aids such as picture captions, maps, graphs, charts and tables.

If a specific fact or facts are needed, the most appropriate reading technique is to skim through the material, using the headings, until the information is located. If children automatically plow laboriously through everything they read, they are in danger of becoming discouraged and giving up, assuming that it is too hard for them.

Children can be shown that they can skim difficult material to find specific information. They should also be taught to record what they find accurately, fully identifying the source (name, date, page).

If the information needed is more complex and conceptual, the children should be taught to skim the material, taking notes (by jotting down phrases, dates and other facts, or full quotes) of anything they select as relevant. They will then need to organize the material according to their purpose, and if they have used several sources, to integrate all the information gathered. This involves selecting main ideas and supporting details. Making an outline helps considerably in this process.

Before the material can actually be used for whatever purpose it was intended (making a written or oral report, participating in a discussion or debate, or just storing it in one's memory for future use), children should try to make some judgment about how good their information is: Do they have enough information for their topic? Is the information accurate—is it current enough, is it factual? If it is an opinion, is it backed up? Are there other opinions that should be reported as well?

This is indeed a formidable array of skills. Not only will the children need ample time and practice in developing them, but the teachers will need to be patient in taking one step at a time, and resourceful in cooperating with each other and with the school librarian to plan appropriate small and big projects for individual students or groups of students.

Steps in Teaching Actually, in teaching children study skills and procedures, and steps in use of reference materials, it is a good idea to take up just one source at a time. Presenting children with a question or a problem will create a need for consulting that particular reference, and then the specific steps in using the source can be explored and demonstrated.

After some activities have sent children into several different types of reference materials and they have become somewhat familiar and proficient in their use, a full-blown research topic can be assigned as a cooperative class project. For example, let us say that the art teacher and the language arts teacher have taken the class to a special exhibit at the museum, and the children have become interested in knowing more about the subject. The teachers and children might together work out an outline of questions they would like to have answered:

What, exactly, is impressionism?
> How is it different from what came before?
> How is it different from what came after?

Where and when did it start?

Why did it start?
> Was it because of a special person?
> Was it because of a special event?

Who were the important people in this new art style?
> The artists they had seen at the exhibit?
> Any others?

The class could get together a bibliography of resources, including the encyclopedia (listing the volumes in which they would find the articles on Impressionism and on each artist), and other volumes they had found listed in the card file under these same topics. Then groups of children could be assigned to research each of the questions in the outline, taking notes. Finally they could pool all their information. They might decide to make an illustrated book with their findings, create a script for a guided lecture tour for students in other classes, submit them to the school newspaper, or just post their articles on a bulletin board.

After small, specific experiences with each reference source, and after participating in a group project, children should be ready for individual study assignments.

These are some topics that have been used to introduce children to each of various reference sources:

What would you give your parents for their 20th anniversary? (This was looked up in the index of the World Almanac under the word anniversary. In the Reader's Digest Almanac there was no listing for anniversary in the index, but the children found it in the Table of Contents under the sub-topic Marriage and Divorce which was under the main topic Home and Family.)

Mary is thinking about which college she would like to go to. She wants a college that is not too big, that is in the northeast, and is not too expensive. (The class looked in the almanac index, under colleges, universities, education, and went through charts that gave location, tuition, and enrollment information. The librarian also recommended that they look into *Lovejoy's College Guide* [Lovejoy, Clarence E., New York, Simon and Shuster, 1974].)

What was Babe Ruth's real name, and when and how did he die? (encyclopedia)

What is the most common first name in the world? (*Guinness Book of World Records*)

Who first said, "To err is human, to forgive, divine"? (*Bartlett's Quotations*)

If Henry Kissinger wanted to give his wife a birthstone ring, what kind would he buy? (*Who's Who in America* and almanac)

Mr. and Mrs. Cantor want to take a trip to Europe. They want to visit the capitals of Italy, France, and England. Also, Mr. Cantor wants to go skiing on Mont Blanc, and Mrs. Cantor, who is a music lover, wants to see Beethoven's birthplace. What cities will they visit and what would be a logical route? (atlas, encyclopedia)

The Dictionary Up until now, the children were exposed to the use of the dictionary for looking up spellings and definitions of words. At the advanced level, the dictionary is treated as a reference source and the following additional uses of the dictionary are established: to find out how to pronounce a word, where the accent should go; to know how to syllabify words; to look up abbreviations, plural forms, tenses; to look up foreign expressions; to find word origins; to recognize word roots, prefixes, and suffixes. In addition to going to the dictionary for these various purposes as they come up during normal reading activities, practice exercises such as the following provide pleasurable drill and pinpoint specific usages:

1. She was somewhat shy and blushed as she went up to <u>present</u> the <u>present</u> to the principal. How do the underlined words differ?
2. You are typing and the last word on the line is *sociology*. You can't fit it all on one line, so what will you do?
3. If I wrote *n.g.* on your homework paper, how would you feel?
4. I know how to dive very well. Yesterday I _____ from the highest diving board.
5. I had only one brother-in-law before. Now my second sister is getting married and I will have two _____ .
6. What would your mother have to do to your pie if you told her you wanted it *a la mode*?
7. The sandwich is probably the most popular American lunch food. Is it an American word? How did it originate?

8. What word would you look for in the dictionary if you wanted to look up these words:

> nimbly
>
> neediest
>
> eaten
>
> reenter
>
> caresses

9. *Inform* is the root of all these words except

> informant   informal   information   misinformed

10. The root *pend* means *hang*. How many words can you list that have this root?

Enjoying Literature

Very often children at the advanced level, in their eagerness to enlarge their information and knowledge, turn to works of non-fiction and have little interest in the various forms of fiction. They are not aware that there may be as much to be learned from a poem, a story, or novel as from a book on science or history. This may be due in part to the way they have been taught; some teachers approach fiction as though it contained a sequence of facts, and on this level it could not compete with a non-fiction work. And, of course, works of literature often present overwhelming language difficulties for deaf children, and the teacher may again lose the ball by automatically turning the reading into a language and vocabulary lesson. Literature can be the source of much language learning, but that should not become the main focus; there are easier, more enjoyable activities that are designed specifically for vocabulary enrichment, whereas the joys of appreciating a work of literature go beyond the vocabulary level.

An inspired literature teacher who loves books and regards reading as one of life's essential functions, like breathing, can do much to enrich the lives of deaf children by introducing them to the riches of thought, experience, and expression awaiting them between the covers of books. I have seen certain teachers working with children on books they themselves love, transmitting magical insight and inspiration. Not all deaf children may be able to respond on this level, but it would be a pity if out of a sense of futility we deprived all of them of the opportunity. By the careful selection of material, by the quality of help extended in reading (which holds children responsible for their highest performance and generously and wisely supplements this as needed), and by focusing on the essence and not the minutae of a book, the teacher can make the reading of an author's work a prized activity. When motivation (teacher's and pupils') is high, and the quality of teaching excels, deaf children can rise to the occasion and exercise vigors of mind and will.

Purposes Over and above all, if the teacher can infuse and inspire children with the purposes of reading literature, they may adopt it as a choice personal activity, and a permanent avenue of growth will have opened up to them. Fiction can serve many functions:

1. Books may be read for sheer entertainment. Some books, such as mysteries, works of humor, adventure, science fiction, fantasy, and romance are designed to provide the reader with temporary relief from the realities and travails of living (which is not to say that these books are never informative as well, or that more serious books are not enjoyable or entertaining). But the major purpose is to divert and amuse, and if these books are read purely at that level, the readers will not be doing themselves, or these books, an injustice. This is no small thing, either. If deaf children can begin to get as much fun from books as from movies, TV, and games, they will have added importantly to their resources. They will have more ways of spending leisure time; being alone will not mean having nothing to do; and they will undoubtedly learn as they are entertained.

2. Books can be the source of important insights, insights into people, events, life. Most works of fiction deal in some way with the human condition, with people under some particular kind of inner or outer stress. Children can learn more about themselves as they learn in books about other people who may share some of their own problems or conditions, or who are faced with dilemmas that are inevitable in life. By sharing the feeling and adventures of book characters, they grow in their appreciation and understanding of the mainsprings of personality and character. Many a story or novel gives as much or more insight into people's motives and behavior than a tome on psychology. The children in one class read "Bang the Drum Slowly" and had some very deep discussions about such major human issues as loyalty, death, courage, self-image. Works of fiction can also give insight into historical events and times. In many cases, an era or event out of the past can be imbued with greater clarity and currency by an author than by a historian. The deaf children who read A Tale of Two Cities and The Diary of Anne Frank acquired a great understanding of the impact of the French Revolution and of the Hitler regime on the people who lived through these epochs.

3. Books can help you develop a personal philosophy or outlook on life. Through books, children can encounter philosophies and ethical values that differ from their own and from those of the people with whom they have direct contact. Underlying every book is a particular point of view about the characters and events described in that book. An author with a body of life experiences and attitudes and values chose to create these particular people and cast them into certain circumstances in order to illustrate some particular concept. When the reader grasps the author's underlying viewpoint, a dialogue or debate can ensue between reader and author. The teacher who encourages children to probe for this depth in reading is helping them develop an understanding of the world and life in general. From time immemorial, people have sought for broader understanding of the meaning and purpose of life. It is possible to seek it in books. Works of literature throw light on such issues as individuality and conformity, freedom and restraint, free will and fate, self-interest and idealism, nature of man, nature of evil, prejudice, jealousy, etc.

4. Books can sharpen your sensitivity to language. It is language that differentiates man from every other form of life. It is through language that we express not only wishes, needs, ideas, but also our particular personalities. Most of the time, deaf children are struggling simply to acquire sufficient linguistic skill for ordinary purposes of communication. Much of the language that deaf children are habitually exposed to is simple, trite, stilted, lacking in color, nuance, or subtlety. At the advanced level many deaf children are ready to go beyond this. Without laboriously teaching language through reading, the sensitive teacher can still give children opportunities for partaking in the pleasure of responding to well-written prose and poetry. Many deaf children enjoy words and can appreciate the beauty of imaginative language, of a good idea clothed in well-chosen words.

Selection The problem of choosing material which is appropriate to the interest level, but not beyond the ability level of the children, is a compelling one and not easily resolved. However, there are some mitigating factors. For one thing, the range of materials available is simply phenomenal. There are works in every literary genre, from the distant past to the present, on every conceivable theme, of varying lengths, in every kind of edition. Another helping factor is that generally at this level the children are more highly motivated. Up until now they were more passive or sponge-like in learning, some absorbing more than others. Now they seem to be more aware and concerned about all the things they don't know and actively seek to learn. Even those children with minimal linguistic skills often hunger for knowledge and information and will work harder at this level. In reading any work of literature, if the teacher focuses on the broad purposes and gives ample help and guidance in plumbing depths of meaning, some of the rewards of literature can be made available to all children. My own tendency is to select materials of very high interest, even if they may be difficult, and pool the group's resources in discussing the work. All the children should have copies of the work. For this type of reading lesson it is preferable if they actually have their own paperback editions which they may annotate. Accumulating a library of read books is a marvelous habit to instill.

With certain children only a few selections will be read together for the enjoyment and understanding of literature. The remainder of their reading program will be devoted to functional and remedial reading activities. With other children, a more thorough survey of literature will be made during the years they spend at this level. These children will more or less systematically take up various forms of literary writings (novel, drama, poetry, short story, biography, essay), and sample works of American, British, and European writers from the past and present. The curriculum of the particular school will determine just how much choice the teacher and the children may exercise.

Analyzing a Literary Work   Whatever work has been chosen for study, the teacher and the children will explore and discuss the plot, the theme, the characterization, and the style. This, of course, calls for the use of all the skills involved in literal and inferential levels of comprehension, as well as critical reading. Different works will require different approaches, but whether the work is contemporary or classic; a short story, play, poem or novel; read in one sitting or over a period of time; the quality of the experience is what matters. The hope is that having had one literary experience that was thorough and both meaningful and enjoyable, there will be motivation to continue. Having been guided in taking from the work both superficial and in-depth meanings, students will have a standard and method to apply on their own.

For example, the librarian and the reading teacher jointly read with one particular class the novel *Ramona* by Helen Hunt Jackson. Some of the sessions took place in the library and some in the classroom. These predominantly white, middle-class, urban children were curious about the world, but needed a background for the reading of a book written in 1883, set in the American Southwest, dealing with the treatment of Indians and Mexicans. Materials on the history of the period and on the life of the author were researched and provided insights and preparation for the book. The children were told that as they read, they might think about what made this book a classic that continues to be read today, while many other books written at that time have vanished. The book was read and discussed over a long period of time. Interest remained at a high pitch because after the plot was summarized, the discussions focused on the characters and their personalities and motivations, and on the relationship between the events in the book to the history of the country at that time. The students talked about what kind of persons the characters were, what their attitudes were, what life forces had formed these attitudes. They substantiated their opinions with references to facts and events described in the book. As they came to know these story people, the students grew to understand them, love them, pity them, sympathize with them. The following excerpts from character sketches written by the students will indicate the depth of their perception.

> Senor Felipe Morena was a very fine gentleman who was fair-minded and honorable. He was really a weak kind of man during his early manhood. He didn't have any determination and often readily agreed with his mother and other people. After awhile he began to understand what lay before him. His character changed and he became a determined man.

> Ramona was a religious and a faithful girl. She respected everyone, even Senora Morena, who was always mean to her. Everyone loved her because she was charming and fun-loving, but as she grew older she was very unhappy. Her courage helped her face many hardships and she was calm and patient through her sufferings.

> Senora Morena, a lovely Spanish girl, was married to General Morena at the age of twenty. After many years of marriage, her husband died and she became a hard-hearted woman. She hated the Indians and the Americans and was narrow-minded. She was a religious

woman, but she was ungenerous and unaffectionate to her foster daughter, Ramona, because of Ramona's Indian blood.

Alessandro was Ramona's beloved husband. He was an Indian who was proud of his father, the chief of the tribe. He hated the white men for the way they treated the Indians.

That these pupils had absorbed the story of Ramona at a far more than superficial level is apparent. Here is one pupil's answer to why the book continues to be read today.

"Ramona" is still popular because it is beautifully written. It also teaches lessons which are important today. The story teaches us how to treat human beings, no matter who you are or to what race you belong. The author tried to make people realize how cruelly the Indians and Mexicans were treated. It is also a magnificent love story.

It was hard work to go through the book this way. But the interest was sustained throughout, and the rewards were great. These pupils had a true literary experience. In being guided to apply their information and skill to the printed page, they extracted from the work a depth of understanding and appreciation which added to their knowledge of life. One such experience is far more worthwhile than the reading of many different works just for plot.

Specific Facets of Literary Appreciation To help prepare children for an in-depth appreciation of literature, it is often helpful to isolate various aspects for study. Exercises and activities can be planned to sensitize students to some of the important elements in literature. Through such activities, as well as through a guided study of a specific work in its entirety, we attempt to give students the skills and techniques for the independent enjoyment of literature. Children have generally had a great deal of work on the plot or overt content of material, observing sequences, interrelating details, inferring causes. Focusing on such elements as characterization, style, and theme can broaden their appreciation of the author's craftsmanship in creating a work of literature.

Characterization Often children react to, identify with, or admire or dislike characters without being able to tell why. Although they respond to the author's characterization, they are not fully aware of how that author managed to achieve exactly that desired response, especially if the characters are not described explicitly or overtly. Alerting them to look for clues to characterization in the speech, habits, and actions with which the author has endowed the story characters heightens children's enjoyment and fills them with respect for the way in which the author carefully builds up detail upon detail for a total effect. In the following exercises, children are encouraged to relate the author's description of details of behavior to their own generalizations about personality.

1. After dinner, they gathered in the living room and chatted gaily in small groups. Only John did not join in the festivities. He sat alone in a corner puffing away at his pipe as though hoping to disappear behind a cloud of smoke. His legs were crossed tightly and one foot bobbed up and down in short, jerky movements. His eyes avoided meeting anyone else's as he stared blankly ahead.

In the opposite corner of the room, all the children had gathered around Pete as though drawn by a magnet. His voice boomed out in merry laughter and his hands were always busy patting a young head or lifting a tot high into the air. His deep bass voice made the story he was telling sound more like a poem or a song. The children's faces glowed with pleasure as he beamed on them.

(a) Write **J** and **P** somewhere along these scales to show how you would rate John and Pete:

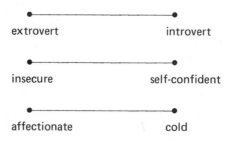

extrovert   introvert

insecure   self-confident

affectionate   cold

(b) Under each scale, jot down words from the paragraph that show why you rated them that way.

(c) If you were told that John and Pete were brothers, what guesses might you make about them—e.g., about their age, their parents?

2. She didn't talk, she purred. She walked as soundlessly as a cat on her rubber-soled shoes. You never heard her coming, but suddenly there she was at your elbow. The saccharine smile never

left her lips, a smile which brightened her mouth but never reached her eyes. Her words seem to have been dipped in honey. "Have you heard what happened to Mrs. Evans?" she asked with her inevitable smile.

"No. Did her husband get that job he was interviewed for?"

"No. You know, he almost had it. They liked him so much and they wanted to hire him. He was so excited. All he had to do before starting on the new job was to take a physical. And you know what? They found that he has a heart murmur."

And as she moved on soundlessly to spread the news to yet another person, her smile hung incongruously in the air.

(a) Which word best describes this character?
  sweet   hypocritical   fussy   happy

(b) Would you trust her? Why?

(c) Would you like her for a friend? Why?

3. Mr. Jack was an old friend of the Lamont family and came to visit now and then. Unfortunately, Mr. Jack was a stutterer and communication with him was somewhat difficult. Mrs. Lamont had told the children that they must never laugh at poor Mr. Jack.

One evening, Mr. Jack was having dinner with the Lamonts. He kept stuttering and stuttering. Mrs. Lamont could sense that the tension was mounting as the children were trying to keep from laughing. Suddenly she herself burst into laughter, "Look what I did," she said. "I just put salt in my coffee instead of sugar!" Everyone was relieved to be able to join in laughing at Mrs. Lamont.

(a) What kind of person was Mrs. Lamont?
  silly   sensitive   funny   careful

(b) What kind of mother is she?
  strict   inconsistent   easygoing   understanding

(c) Would you like her for a friend? Why?

4. He was a man of 60, handsomely dressed, haughty in manner and with a face like a fine mask. A face of transparent paleness; every feature in it clearly defined; one set expression on it. The nose, beautifully formed otherwise, was very slightly pinched at the top of each nostril. These two compressions in the nose persisted in changing colour sometimes, and they would be occasionally dilated and contracted by something like a faint pulsation; then they gave a look of treachery and cruelty to the whole countenance. Examined

with attention its capacity of helping such a look was to be found in the line of the mouth.

(a) What do you think this man would say if he were riding in a carriage and some people got in its way? Now read the rest of this selection. Were you almost right?

With a wild rattle and clatter, the carriage dashed through streets with women screaming before it and men clutching children out of its way. "You dogs!" said the Marquis, but smoothly and with an unchanged front except as to the spots on his nose. "I would ride over any of you very willingly and exterminate you from the earth."[1]

(b) What do you think the Marquis would say if a friend asked him for a loan?

(c) What do you think John and Pete (selection 1), the woman in selection 2, and Mrs. Lamont (selection 3) might say if a friend asked them for a loan?

Theme Children need a great deal of help, experience, and practice in order to be able to generalize the theme of a work of literature, and to perceive and understand the author's point of view and philosophy of life. As was indicated, it is very helpful when a selection is being studied to get some background information about the author and the time he or she lived in or wrote about.

Selections using fables, myths, and folk tales which involve children in examining and discussing differing attitudes, perspectives, and opinions can prepare them for the kind of conceptualization needed to reach profounder levels of the author's theme. The following are examples of short, concrete passages that can be used to lead children to examine more abstract issues.

1. If you have three different things to eat on your plate, do you eat the one you like best first, or last? Do you tend to think more about the present, or to worry about the future?

The Crawfords and the Armstrongs live on neighboring farms. Every fall each family fills a barrel with apples from their farm and puts it in the cellar for the winter. Every week during the winter, Mrs. Crawford sends her son, Robert, down to the cellar for some apples. She tells him to choose the apples that are beginning to turn brown.

[1] Dickens, Charles. *A Tale of Two Cities*

Mrs. Armstrong also sends her son down to their cellar to get apples for the week. But she tells him to choose the nicest, shiniest, reddest apples. So, all winter long, the Armstrongs eat good apples, and the Crawfords eat apples that are going bad.

(a) Which family lives for the present? Which family lives for the future?

(b) Which family is more like your own?

(c) Does the writer of this story sympathize with the Armstrongs or with the Crawfords?

2. Do you think about growing old? Do you look forward to growing older, or do you dread it? Writers and philosophers have done a lot of thinking about age, but they do not always agree. Here are some examples of what some people have said about it:

> Youth is a silly, vapid state;
> Old age with fears and ills is rife;
> This simple boon I beg of Fate—
> A thousand years of Middle Life!
> Carolyn Wells

Old age, believe me, is a good and pleasant time. It is true that you are gently shouldered off the stage, but then you are given such a comfortable front stall as spectator, and, if you have really played your part, you are more content to sit down and watch.
Jane Ellen Harrison

Old age, especially an honored old age, has so great authority, that this is of more value than all the pleasures of youth.
Cicero

Solon was under a delusion when he said that a man when he grows old may learn many things—for he can no more learn much than he can run much; youth is the time for extraordinary toil.
Plato

(a) If you were old, which quotations would you find comforting? Which would you find disturbing?

(b) Which quotation do you like best? Which do you agree with most?

(c) If you could stop the clock when you reached the age you like best, where would you stop it?

3. Some famous people, such as Abraham Lincoln and Jesus, used to be fond of telling stories when they wanted to make a point. The stories would make you laugh sometimes, but they made you think.

> This story is an old, old parable. It is about a man who lived in a small village in Europe. He had a wife, several children, and many problems. He worked hard, but was very poor.
>
> All his life he wanted to see the big City, but he could not afford to go there. But one night he just decided to go. He left his wife and children and his house and started walking to the City. Pretty soon he came to a forest. It was night so he decided to stop and go to sleep. He took off his shoes and put them under a tree, pointing them in the direction he would have to take to get to the City.
>
> He didn't know it, but in the middle of the night someone turned his shoes around. In the morning, he woke up, put on his shoes and started walking in the direction they had been pointing. Pretty soon he came to what he thought was the big City.
>
> "That's very funny," he thought. "This city looks just like my own." He walked and walked and was surprised to find everything very familiar. Soon he came to a house that looked just like his own house, with a woman who looked just like his wife, and children who looked just like his children.
>
> So he stayed there. But now he was no longer restless or discontent. Wherever he went, he thought, things would always be the same.
>
> (a) Do you think this man would have been happy if he had reached the City?
>
> (b) Was it a good thing that he went away? Would he have finally been content if he had never gone away?
>
> (c) Do you agree with him that things would be the same no matter where he was?
>
> (d) George Moore has said, "A man travels the world over in search of what he needs and returns home to find it." Do you agree with this?
>
> (e) When people are discontent, sometimes they try to change the conditions outside themselves, and sometimes they try to change the ideas and feelings inside themselves. Which do you think is better?

Style It is likely that developing an appreciation of style, or a sensitivity to language, is the most elusive of all skills (not only for deaf children, but for hearing children as well). Yet, for those children at the advanced level who are ready for this, it can be very worthwhile. Although the emphasis is on promoting receptive understanding of certain linguistic devices rather than on stimulating expressive use, deaf children will often surprise you by trying to use creative language to make their own communication more colorful.

Most of the time, the teacher will try to point out particularly apt uses of words or linguistic devices in whatever is being read. If an author is distinguished by a particular stylistic habit, this will be called to the children's attention (e.g., Damon Runyon's use of fractured English in dialogue, Salinger's colloquial autobiographic stream of consciousness, O. Henry's surprise endings).

In addition, specific activities and exercises will be introduced to acquaint children with standard techniques of imagery in style. Children will enjoy making up special vocabulary books collecting their own examples of imaginative uses of typical devices.

1. Figures of speech—simile, metaphor, personification, alliteration. A source that is very accessible to children is to be found in the lyrics of current folk and rock songs.

> *I wanted magic shows and miracles*
> *Mirages to touch* (Pippin)

> *Some men are born to live at ease*
> *Doing what they please*
> *Richer than the bees are in honey*
> (Godspell)

And, of course, the classics provide an endless supply of effective writing using imagery.

> It was a rimy morning, and very damp. I had seen the damp lying on the outside of my little window, as if some goblin had been crying there all night, and using the window for a pocket-handkerchief.
> (Great Expectations)

> Her heart was like the soles of those shoes. Wealth and luxury had rubbed against it and left upon it something that would never wear away.
> (Madame Bovary)

2. Picturesque words and expressions. The children will enjoy seeing how expression is enhanced by replacing a bland word with a more colorful one.

> torn — ragged
> tight — clinging
> complained — grumbled
> dry — parched, bone-dry
> said — chirped

3. Collecting idioms, colloquialisms, slang expressions, manners of speech.

4. Listing descriptive words and phrases under the different senses.

> smell — aroma, stench, pungent, rancid
> touch — clammy, vise-like grip, clutch
> sound — blood-curdling, murmur, bellow, discordant
> taste — succulent, lumpy, acrid
> sight — gaunt, loose-limbed, slouch, frail

5. Drawing pictures (or posing for or enacting scenes) to illustrate selections with picturesque or well-chosen detail.

> At last the passengers dropped off to sleep, some with their mouths wide open, others with their chins on their breasts, leaning against their neighbours' shoulders or lolling with their arms through the strap, lurching from side to side with the swaying of the vehicle; and the reflection of the lantern, which swung to and fro outside cast blood-red shadows on all these tranquil sleepers.   (Madame Bovary)

Skill Building

Reading skills need to be rapidly and intensively developed at the advanced level. Those students who will be going on to higher education will need mature reading skills for the tasks ahead. And for those children who may be terminating their formal education with their completion of the work at the advanced level, this may be their last chance to acquire help with needed skills. In addition to working on skill building while using all the usual reading materials, special exercises to focus on specific aspects of reading should be provided. For best results, these should not be just dull drill but should be interesting in and of themselves.

Comprehension—For all groups, but especially for the children who are trying to close the language-reading gap, providing materials with easier language than is found in the usual reading matter at this level permits greater concentration on reading for comprehension.

1. This story was adapted from an actual newspaper item:

Cathie Price is a 15-year-old girl who is crazy about animals. But she is allergic to fur and feathers. So instead of the usual cat or dog or parakeet for a pet, Cathie raises snakes.

She started her unusual hobby when she was 10 years old, at a Girl Scout camp, when Cathie and a group of friends found a nest of garter snakes under a log.

While most of the other girls ran off shrieking, Cathie thought the snakes were just "wonderful" and decided to take some home.

Her present collection lives in a large wooden box in the back yard of the family home. It includes 20 garter snakes, five dekays and one baby water snake.

She explains that it is difficult to obtain food for her pets in the winter. "The only hitch," says Cathie, "is that this particular group of snakes eats only toads and frogs. It's pretty hard to keep a supply on hand."

Her family and friends, she says, are "divided in their opinion" about her pets.

She lists her Dad and two younger brothers as supporters. Her mother, however, prefers that the snakes keep their distance, and her 17-year-old sister is "plain scared to death of them."

Among those who don't share her enthusiasm for snakes is a neighbor who once threatened to "do away with them."

(a) A good title for this story would be
    Scaring the Neighbors
    Snakes in the Back Yard
    A Perfect Hobby for Cathie
    The Family Pet
(b) Why does Cathie have snakes instead of more common pets?
(c) How long has she had her unusual hobby?
(d) How did she get her first pet snake?
(e) How many does she have now?
(f) Where does she keep them?
(g) When does Cathie have trouble taking care of her pets? Why?
(h) How many people are there in Cathie's family?
(i) Who is the oldest child?
(j) Does the oldest like the snakes?
(k) Do Cathie's brothers like the snakes?

    (l)   How do her parents feel about the snakes?

    (m) How do the neighbors like Cathie's pets?

2. Harry Cole came home from a party at 2 a.m. He had had a wonderful time, but was very tired now. He dropped into bed, looking forward to a good night's sleep. But he tossed and turned and couldn't fall asleep. Some noise kept disturbing him and preventing him from getting to sleep.

Suddenly he had an idea about what to do about it. He picked up the telephone and dialed the number of his next-door neighbor. A woman answered the phone.

"Hello, Mrs. Malcolm," said Harry. "Can I please speak to your husband?"

"At this hour!" Mrs. Malcolm exclaimed. "He's asleep."

"I know, but it's very, very important," Harry insisted.

"Oh, all right. Just a minute and I'll wake him up."

As soon as Harry heard Mrs. Malcolm waking Mr. Malcolm up, he hung up. He didn't wait to talk to him. Then he went back to bed and fell right asleep.

Why did Harry want to wake Mr. Malcolm up?

(Answer: He was snoring so loud it kept Harry from sleeping.)

3. One day two men were traveling through a forest together. It was getting dark and they were a little frightened. They said to each other, "Let us promise to stick together in case of danger."

Soon a bear came out of the woods. One of the men immediately climbed up a tree, forgetting all about his friend. The other man couldn't climb so he lay flat on the ground face down, holding his breath. He remembered that a bear will not touch dead meat. The bear came up to the man and sniffed at him. The man lay absolutely stiff and still, not moving a muscle, not even breathing. Soon the bear went away, leaving the man unharmed.

The first man then came down from the tree. "I saw the bear sniffing at you. Did he harm you?" he asked.

"Oh, no," said his traveling companion. "He just whispered in my ear never to trust a coward or I would always be betrayed."

    (a) A good title for this story is

        A Good Friend

        Fooling a Bear

        Betrayed

    (b) This story teaches a lesson. What moral does it show?

One good deed deserves another.

Never count on a friend.

A friend in need is a friend indeed.

(c) Complete the outline.

I. Where the story takes place:

II. The characters in the story:

III. The action:

What the men promise:

Who appears:

What one man does:

What the other man does:

What the bear does:

IV. Moral of the story:

(d) How did each man save his own life?

(e) Who showed quick thinking?

(f) How did the men feel toward each other after the bear incident?

(g) How could they have helped each other?

(h) Which man would you choose to travel with?

4. A Test of Wisdom

Long, long ago in the land of Israel there ruled a king who was known all over the world for his wisdom. King Solomon was thought to be the wisest man who ever lived. People came to his court from all over in order to learn from him.

In the land of Sheba, there ruled a queen who was very beautiful and who admired wisdom very much. She heard about King Solomon and she made up her mind that she must go and see for herself if he was indeed as wise as everyone said.

So the Queen set forth for Israel. When she arrived in Jerusalem, the capital of Israel, King Solomon greeted her warmly and gave a big feast in her honor.

The next day the king was holding his court of justice, where people came to him with their quarrels and their problems. The Queen of Sheba had decided to test Solomon's wisdom.

She came before the court and placed two wreaths of flowers on a little table before the king.

"Great king," she said, "The whole world has heard of your wisdom. I have here two garlands of flowers. They look exactly the same, but the flowers of one garland are real, and the flowers of the other garland are artificial. Can you tell which garland is real and which is false?"

The court was very silent as everyone watched the king, for the garlands really looked exactly alike. He stared at the garlands for a minute. Then he smiled and walked over to the window. He opened it and a little bee flew into the room from the garden outside. It did not hesitate but flew right to one of the garlands and settled on it.

"There is your real garland," said the King.

(a) Did you get the main idea of the story?
What do you think the Queen of Sheba said at the end?

(b) How carefully do you read?
King Solomon was known all over the world for his:
courage wisdom kindness
The Queen of Sheba went to King Solomon's court:
to test the King
to marry the King
to give the King a garland
The Queen made the garlands:
as a present for the King
to show off her beauty and wisdom
to fool the King
The King found which was the real garland:
by smelling them
by asking the Queen
by seeing which one the bee chose

(c) True or false:
King Solomon was supposed to be wise but he really wasn't.
Sheba is the name of a Queen.
Jerusalem is a city in Sheba.
The garlands looked exactly the same.
The garlands were exactly the same.
The Queen did not fool the King.

(d) Do you remember the facts?
Where did King Solomon live?
What was he famous for?
Why did the Queen of Sheba go to Israel?
How did the Queen test the King?
How did the King find the real garland?

(e) Vocabulary
Find two places where the word *court* is used. Do they mean the same thing? Which one means a place where

law trials are held? Which one means a royal palace?

Find the phrase *made up her mind* in the story. Now find a word in another part of the story that means the same thing.

Find another word in the story that means *garlands.*

Find another word in the story that means *artificial.*

When you *admire* something, you
   like it
   dislike it

When you say *indeed*, you mean
   yes
   no

When you *set forth* for someplace, you
   start out
   come back
   arrive

Following Directions
1. **A Trick.** Can you cut a 3″ x 4″ piece of paper so that you can make a necklace that you can get your head through?
Solution
Fold the paper in half lengthwise.

Starting at the folded side, cut slits in the paper about 1/4″ apart. Cut from the folded side to about 1/8″ from the opposite side.

Now turn the paper upside down so that the folded edge is away from you. Cut another series of slits in between the first series of cuts. These slits should also stop 1/8″ away from the opposite edge.

Now cut along the fold, but be very careful not to cut the first slit or the last slit.

Unfold the paper gently. It is big enough to go over your head.

4″

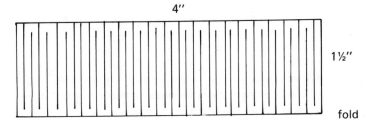

1½″

fold

2. A Puzzle

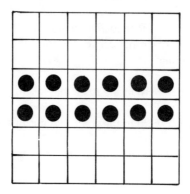

Can you rearrange the checkers so that there are only two in each line vertically, horizontally or diagonally?

Solution

Put one checker in each of the four corners.

In the second row from the top, put two checkers in the two middle boxes.

In the third row, put one checker in the second square from the left, and one checker in the second square from the right.

Do the same in the fourth row.

In the fifth row, do the same as you did in the second row.

3. A Logical Riddle

Mr. Brown, Mr. Green and Mr. Black were having lunch together. One wore a brown necktie, one a green tie, one a black.

"Have you noticed," said the man with the green tie, "that our ties have colors that match our names, but not one of us has on a tie that matches his own name."

"By golly, you're right!" exclaimed Mr. Brown.

What color tie was each man wearing?

Solution

Mr. Brown could not be wearing a brown tie. He was not wearing a green tie because the man who talked to him was. So Mr. Brown must have been wearing a black tie.

The man with the green tie could not have been Mr. Green. Nor was he Mr. Brown. So he must be Mr. Black.

That leaves a brown tie for Mr. Green.

4. A Puzzle

Although Mr. and Mrs. Jones have five children, they never forget their birthdays. They have a very interesting way to remember exactly when each child was born.

The children's first names tell what month they were born in. The first and last letters are the same as the first and last letters of the month.

Their middle names tell the date and the year of their birth, if you change the letters into numbers. The first letter tells the date, and the last two letters tell the year.

Here are the children's names. Figure out their birth dates:

Fanny Efa Jones	(February 5, 1961)
Jerome Ted Jones	(June 20, 1954)
Murray Jef Jones	(May 10, 1956)
Oliver Reg Jones	(October 18, 1957)
Oscar Reg Jones	(October 18, 1957)

Why do Oliver and Oscar have the same middle names? (They are twins.)

Who is the youngest?	(Fanny)
Who is the oldest?	(Jerome)
How much older than Fanny is Murray?	(3 years, 3½ months)

If the Jones had a baby who was born on July 8, 1970, what could they name it?

Language

At the advanced level, children who have already acquired minimal linguistic skills will be able to promote their own language through reading. The materials they read will be an endless source of new vocabulary, and if they read enough, they will be better able to handle more complicated linguistic constructions. Word play at this level can be a very delightful route to linguistic facility. The exercises that follow build dexterity in handling phonemes, adverbs, prefixes and suffixes, prepositions, punctuation, phrase constructions. Mistakes in language which change meanings and become the source of jokes and laughter sometimes teach more memorably than the most carefully organized lessons.

1. Phonemes   A spoonerism is a funny mistake people sometimes make when they accidently switch around the letters of different words. For example, if instead of saying *forks and spoons*, you said *sporks and foons*, that would be a spoonerism. The word spoonerism comes from the name of a British clergyman, William Archibald Spooner. He was probably a little self-conscious in speaking because he often mixed his words up, making funny mistakes. Here are some spoonerisms. Can you figure out what they are really supposed to say?

Is your TV color or whack and blight?
He has a sin twister.
President Hoobert Herver
The Duck and Dooches of Windsor.
He is a newted nose analyst.
Shellout falters.
A roaring pain is falling outside.
It is kisstomary to cuss the bride.
He's not as smart as some theeple pink.

The Rev. Mr. Spooner is supposed to have said to a lady in church, "Mardon me, padam, but this pie is occupewed. May I sew you to another sheet?" What did he really mean?

2. **Adverbs** In each of the following sentences the adverb fits another word in the sentence so well that it is funny. Can you find the word that the adverb goes with?

"I've got to get a new tire," he said flatly.
"I'm only three feet tall," he said shortly.
"I've lived in the desert for five years," he said dryly.
"The man is dead," she said lifelessly.

Choose the adverb from the list below that fits each of these sentences.

"This knife is sharp," she said _____ .
"I wasn't even in school that day," he said _____ .
"May I have some sugar?" she said _____ .
"It's absolutely freezing in here," he said _____ .
"I hope this is the end," she said _____ .
"That seems very odd to me," he said _____ .
"Oh, what a beautiful lamp," she said _____ .
"It's impossible to bend this," he said _____ .

sweetly	icily
finally	brightly
stiffly	evenly
absently	cuttingly

3. **Prefixes and Suffixes** Sometimes adding prefixes or suffixes to words changes their meaning a great deal. In these sentences, add a prefix to the underlined word to make the sentence say the opposite of what it says now.

My brother suddenly <u>appeared</u>.
It was <u>fair</u> of the teacher to punish the class.
This furniture is made of <u>war</u> materials.
The parents were <u>informed</u> about the new rules.
My mother was <u>pleased</u> with my report card.

Sometimes prefixes and suffixes change the word meaning only slightly. But they do change the way the word is used in the sentence. For example, these two sentences have the same meaning but the sentence forms are different.

Tomorrow is the day I graduate from school.
Tomorrow is my graduation day at school.

Rewrite the following sentences, but do not change the meaning. Use a different suffix for the underlined word.

Jose has a great <u>interest</u> in sports.
I <u>teach</u> deaf children.
Mary is full of <u>mischief.</u>
Next week is John's <u>initiation</u> into the fraternity.
Muriel got an award for <u>attending</u> school every day.

4. **Sarcasm** Sometimes people say something, but you can tell from the way they say it that they mean just the opposite of what they are saying. This is called sarcasm. The way you know when people are being sarcastic is by noticing which word they are emphasizing. Usually if you change that word to its opposite, you will get the real meaning.

Match each of these sentences to the scene it probably goes with. Then find the word that was used sarcastically and change it to its opposite.

I must go see what those sweet little children are up to.
I really picked a good time to do my homework.
I just love the way you took care of your clothing.
I'm certainly glad you offered to help me.

Family excitedly watching prizefight on TV.
Mother unpacking messy suitcase.
Boy drying dishes and dropping them.
Children playing tag in bedroom.

5. **Pronouns, prepositions, phrases** Jokes, as has been pointed out before, are a wonderful source for developing flexibility in using multiple meanings. They are also a good source for other kinds of word play. A few examples follow:

Two men were working together building a barn. "I'll hold the rivet and when I nod my head, you hit it with the hammer," said the first man to his friend. His friend did as he was told, and the first man saw stars for two weeks.

When the first man said "hit it," what did he mean?

What did his friend think he meant?

A girl bought 50 stamps for her Christmas cards. "Do I have to paste them all on myself?" she asked the postal clerk.

"Heavens, no! You paste them on the envelopes," he answered.

What small word could the girl have used between *on* and *myself* to make herself clear?

Q. Would you rather have a lion eat you or a tiger?

Usual answer: Neither.

Better answer: I'd rather have the lion eat the tiger than eat me.

Police said that between four and five thieves took part in the robbery. (Did you ever see 4½ thieves?)

The owner of the pet shop said proudly, "I have never had a complaint from a single pet that we have sold." (Did you ever see a dog complain?)

Advertisement: New on the market—a shaver for women with three heads. (Did you ever see a three-headed woman?)

At three years of age my father was killed in the war. (Would you believe, a three-year-old father?)

The door opened and a woman carrying a baby and her husband entered. (Must have been a strong woman!)

I'll do it right now.

I'll do it right, now.

Who's in a hurry? Who made a mistake?

He quit, promising he would pay his debts.
He quit promising he would pay his debts.
 Who would you rather have owe you money?

The man said his son is guilty.
"The man," said his son, "is guilty."
 Which son is a lawbreaker?

Who's cooking Mother?
Who's cooking, Mother?
 Which Mother is in trouble?

She stopped wondering whether she was doing the right thing.
She stopped, wondering whether she was doing the right thing.
 Which girl is still having moral conflicts?

Critical Reading

In building comprehension skills, the goal has been to fully grasp the author's overt and implied thoughts. In developing critical reading, the goal is to stimulate children to explore their own thoughts in response to what they read. This means that the material must not only be fully comprehended, but that the content and intent be evaluated and judged. This involves a mature reading level. Most deaf children will not attain this level of performance at this point in their school careers, but they should be started on this road if they are ultimately to grow into it. Too often deaf adults (like many other people) are so in awe of the printed word that they believe everything they read must necessarily be accepted as true. They should be reassured about the validity of their own reactions, and encouraged to compare and judge what they read against their own knowledge, experience, opinions, and standards.

The teacher will have been developing critical attitudes in reading all along by encouraging children to identify the author's point of view, to judge how adequately it has been presented, and to what extent they agree or disagree with it. In addition, specific exercises and activities may be introduced to promote critical attitudes, such as distinguishing between fact and opinion, judging how adequately opinions have been supported by objective facts, detecting the values that underly different opinions and points of view. Some examples follow.

1. **Newspaper reading**   The periodicals specifically designed for school children that were used all along in the reading curriculum have familiarized children to a large extent with the nature, contents, and use of newspapers. But at this level it is important to examine general circulation newspapers, particularly those the parents of the children habitually subscribe to. Children should learn to interpret headlines. They should learn the differences between news items, feature stories, and editorials. They should become familiar with the various sections of a newspaper—ads, obituaries, sports and other regular columns, book, radio and TV reviews, letters to the editor, etc. Assignments such as the following are very helpful:

- (a) Comparing a news item and an editorial on the same topic in the same newspaper.
- (b) Comparing different opinions about a topic expressed in letters to the editor and in columnists' reports in the same newspaper on the same day.
- (c) Comparing news items on the same topic in different newspapers.
- (d) Comparing editorials (or book or movie reviews) about the same topic in different newspapers.
- (e) Comparing front-page headlines in different newspapers on the same day.
- (f) Comparing the number of pictures in different newspapers.
- (g) Comparing the amount of space devoted to foreign, domestic, local, non-political coverage in different newspapers.

2. **Making a study of advertisements**   Collecting and analyzing ads for different products, and for the same products, to see what selling claims and techniques are used (e.g., snob appeal, scientific facts, promises, endorsements). Evaluating good and bad ads from the point of view of esthetic appeal and content (art work, headlines, layout).

3. **Examining different magazines**   Children should become familiar with the wide variety of magazines of a general and special nature so that they may eventually become subscribers, and so that they have some idea of how to use magazines as reference sources. Different types of magazines should be examined for content and readability—news magazines (such as *Time*, *Newsweek*); magazines of political, literary and social comment (*New York, New Yorker, Reader's Digest, Esquire,* etc.); fashion and so-called women's magazines (*House and Garden, Good Housekeeping, Seventeen,*

Parents, etc.); reference magazines (*TV Guide, Cue, Consumers Union Reports,* etc.); special interest magazines (*Dog World, Sports Illustrated, Auto Mechanic,* etc.). If possible, children should try to examine the magazines to see what readership they appeal to (in terms of ads, topics for articles and stories, authors, language level, etc.), and what editorial policy they represent (who the staff is, who the regular contributors are, etc.).

4. **Comparing several different works of fiction** and non-fiction that deal with the same subject. For example, comparing the pages that deal with the Civil War in the class's history textbook with a biography of Abraham Lincoln, and with *Gone With the Wind* and *Uncle Tom's Cabin,* and discussing which were interesting, which were informative, similarities and differences in the opinions, points of view and areas of emphasis.

5. **Holding debates and discussions** on a topic of current interest (e.g., abortion, mercy killing, capital punishment, home relief payments). Collecting materials and information on the topic, and analyzing the opinions represented and the facts presented in support of these opinions.

6. **Presenting selections for class discussion and analysis,** such as the following:

(a) *The following items appeared in the Letters to the Editor column of a newspaper a few days after a news item had reported that a 23-year-old prisoner who was out on parole after serving two years of his sentence had robbed and killed an elderly person.*

The recent outbreak of crimes against the elderly is a disgrace to our city. It can be blamed to a large extent on those softhearted people, including many judges and social workers, who feel so sorry for the underprivileged members of society that they forgive them for everything, even for the most horrible crimes.

Laws are necessary for the protection of society. Everybody, including the underprivileged, must obey these laws. People who break these laws must be severely punished in order to set an example to others. When criminals are allowed to go free, the crime rate rises and everybody lives in fear. The more severe the punishment, the more crimes are prevented. The role of the courts is not to make up for any past injustices suffered by lawbreakers, but to protect the innocent. A criminal should receive a fair trial and if found guilty, severely punished for his crime. His misdeeds should not be overlooked because he suffers from an unfortunate background.

E.B.

It would be unfortunate if the recent slaying of an elderly person by a paroled prisoner made people call for stricter punishment for offenders. I am not defending this crime; it was horrendous, and senseless. But to start punishing all criminals without mercy because of this would also be senseless. It is a proved fact that punishment does not prevent crime no matter how severe the punishment may be. Crime is caused by poverty and ignorance, and if we want to wipe out crime we must wage war on poverty. Punishment merely hardens criminals and makes them even more angry with a society that treats them so badly. We must try to reeducate prisoners by retraining them to become useful citizens. Then they will respect the law instead of breaking it.

J.R.

How do the two writers differ in their opinions about
    crime and punishment?
Do the writers support their opinions with facts?
What kinds of facts would the writers need to prove
    their opinions were right?
Which writer do you agree with? Why?

(b) What is the difference between a fact, a superstition, and a proverb? Next to each sentence tell what the statement is, and whether you agree with it.
    Absence makes the heart grow fonder.
    Out of sight, out of mind.
    Thirteen is an unlucky number.
    Thirteen is an uneven number.
    There's a pot of gold at the end of the rainbow.
    There's a rainbow in the sky when the sun shines
        and it rains all at the same time.

(c) There was an accident in which a taxicab hit a pedestrian. These are the statements that the pedestrian and the cab driver gave the policeman:

"I came out of my office building on 32nd Street and started walking toward the railroad station. I checked the bank clock and noted that it was 2:10. My train didn't leave until 2:40 so I had plenty of time. When the light turned green, I slowly started across 7th Avenue. This cab came speeding along and hit me."

"I was cruising along 7th Avenue and stopped for a light on 33rd Street. When the light changed, I started my cab up again; and just as

I was passing 32nd Street, this man came running across the street. I was going slow, so I braked and only barely hit him."

Compare the facts given by each.

Can you tell which facts are true and which are untrue?

Can you tell who was right?

How could you get more information, or check on the information given?

Reading As a Permanent Interest

From my point of view, it is unnecessary and uninformative to judge the reading program by the scores children achieve on reading tests. Ultimately, you will know how effective the reading program has been by seeing how much satisfaction children derive from reading. If children want to read, and if they can understand what they want to read, the program has succeeded. I certainly would like to see the millennium reached, with all deaf children achieving full literacy. But I know that at this point that is as unrealistic a goal for all deaf children as it would be for all hearing children. Reading is an extraordinarily difficult achievement for deaf children. There will be some children who achieve full literacy, as measured by reading tests, by the time they complete their formal education, and there will be many children who do not.

I would like to suggest that until we reach that state of knowledge that enables us to surmount our present limitations in dealing with the problems of children who do not achieve minimal linguistic skills (and who therefore never achieve more than 4th or 5th grade reading levels on tests), we use more practical, reality-based criteria for judging reading competency. Although I am grieved that so many deaf children do so poorly on reading tests, I am less concerned about what children do with reading tests than I am about what they do with reading materials. I do not really regard children who score 8th grade or above on reading tests, but who never read voluntarily, as fully literate. The reading program has failed not just when it did not succeed in teaching children to fully understand the printed word, but when it failed to inspire children to love the printed word and to make reading an important activity in their lives.

All deaf children will not learn to read equally well, but all deaf children can learn to read what they must read for sheer survival; and all deaf children can find that some areas in their lives will be enhanced by reading. These are fairly realistic goals that all teachers and all deaf children can achieve. Rather than using a flat reading achievement score, the skill of the teacher and the effectiveness of the program can be measured by whether all children can achieve minimal functional reading and then reach beyond that to find whatever joys lie in reading for their particular abilities and interests.

To achieve these goals—the ability to read efficiently whatever functional materials they *must* read, and to read habitually and voluntarily any other reading matter that meets their interests— teachers must be skillful and knowledgeable, and students must be skilled and inspired. A willing, eager, well-prepared student can overcome obstacles. A teacher who is a model of an enthusiastic, discriminating reader, who has a basic knowledge of techniques of teaching reading, and an objective appreciation of the difficulties in store for deaf children, can build an interesting, flexible program that meets the individual needs of different children. To teach all children minimal reading skills and to enable all children to find satisfaction in some area of reading, the teacher must include all types of reading materials in the program and give each child the widest possible range of choice.

Some children will master most of the basic skills in reading and will not only achieve full literacy, but will adopt reading as a choice hobby. These children will continue all their lives to learn and to grow through reading. They will sometimes read for fun, for the pure joy of escape, and sometimes to broaden their knowledge and information about people, places, and ideas in the world beyond their immediate direct experience. The reading program that has succeeded in doing this for children has fulfilled one of the most important roles of education. ☐

APPENDIX A

Outline of Major Developmental Goals

Preschool	Primary	Intermediate	Advanced
Experiences to build concepts	Sight vocabulary	Reading in larger units	Functional literacy
Stimulation of oral language	Word recognition	Reading varied materials for different purposes	Work-study skills
Reading readiness	Phrase and sentence reading	Independent reading	Critical reading
			Appreciation of literature

APPENDIX B

Reading Skills Check List

These skills are cumulative as well as sequential. That is, each successive level assumes a mastery of skills at previous levels. The progression should be: steadily increasing sight vocabulary, greater flexibility in word attack, more independent and mature habits of comprehension.

Preschool
Will sit through a storytelling session
Remembers and dramatizes story sequence
"Reads" books spontaneously
Good visual discrimination—detects gross and minute
    similarities and differences
Recognizes own name in print
Attempts to write name

Primary
Enjoys storytelling sessions, anticipates what will happen
Recognizes familiar common words at sight
Uses picture, configuration, and context clues for
    unfamiliar words
Sounds out initial letters
Understands simple material with known language
Reads in phrase units
Visualizes what is read—can illustrate or
    dramatize to show comprehension
Enjoys choosing and looking through library books
Uses picture dictionary to look up spelling
Knows alphabet (sequence, names, and sounds of
    letters)

Intermediate
Rapidly increasing sight vocabulary
Examines unfamiliar words carefully:
    Looks for familiar parts in words
    Breaks word into syllables
    Tries to sound out words
    Uses context clues plus some linguistic clues

Reads ideas, not words
Reads beyond the words—anticipates, interrelates, infers
Can answer questions about content even when
language of the questions differs from the
language in the text
Enjoys reading independently
Uses dictionary to find meanings of unknown words,
can select appropriate meanings

Advanced
Takes an interest in responsibility for learning
and retaining new vocabulary
Uses many strategies to tackle new words:
Context
Phonic analysis (syllabification, accent,
sounding out vowels as well as consonants)
Structural analysis (root, prefix, suffix)
Grammatic analysis (part of speech, form
class, markers)
Dictionary (word origin, multiple meanings,
pronunciation)
Reads (and understands differences between)
different kinds of materials:
Classic and modern literature—plot, characters,
author's theme, style
Poetry and drama—beauty and economy of
expression, figures of speech
Content materials—organizes material into main
ideas and supporting details; distinguishes
fact from opinion; follows both chronological
and topical sequence; understands causal and
other relationships
Reads carefully materials in science and math—
can follow directions precisely, understands
what is given or known and what is asked,
formulates hypotheses, tests out results and
conclusions
Has working knowledge about content and organization
of various references sources (dictionary, atlas,
almanac, encyclopedia, textbooks, guides, etc.)

Can use: card catalog, index, table of contents,
glossary, charts, maps, graphs

Tries to do independent research—choosing appropriate
sources, taking notes, organizing ideas, writing
reports

Can answer questions on what was read (factual and
interpretive)

Has formed personal tastes and independent habits in
reading

Reads voluntarily

APPENDIX C

Reading Problems Check List

1. Limited sight vocabulary
2. Erratic sight vocabulary—sometimes knows word, other times doesn't know same word
3. Has trouble remembering new words
4. Has trouble learning abstract words
5. Skips over unknown words without attempting to figure them out
6. "Reads" all words without differentiating between known and unknown words
7. Guesses wildly at words using general configuration or key feature
8. Doesn't examine words carefully enough, mistakes words that are similar (e.g., *present* and *parent*)
9. Has poor visual discrimination (e.g., *b* and *d* confusion)
10. Doesn't use context clues
11. Doesn't relate spoken sound to written sound
12. Doesn't group words into phrase or idea units
13. Even when language is known, reads isolated words without visualizing ideas
14. Reads lexical (content) words only, doesn't take meaning from the structural (grammatic) elements
15. Doesn't understand question forms
16. Isolates each sentence, doesn't relate from one sentence to the next, doesn't integrate, anticipate
17. Reads short passages only, is frustrated by longer selections
18. Understands simple language but can't handle complex language
19. Understands concrete language but can't handle abstractions
20. Needs constant help and guidance, cannot read independently
21. Has insufficient grasp of language; in reading, constantly meets new language, seriously interfering with comprehension
22. Doesn't enjoy reading; hardly ever chooses to read on own

APPENDIX D

2. synonyms

```
¹H A ²N D W ³R I ⁴T I N G
      E       I     E
      A       C     S
      T      ⁵H ⁶A T E
              N
           ⁷M I S T A K E
              W
          ⁸B R E A K
              R
```

3. function

```
              ¹D
²S U ³S P E N D E R S
     T       R
    ⁴J E E ⁵P R     ⁶L
     T    ⁷O P T I C I A N
     H    I        C       D
     O    S       ⁸K I L L J O Y
⁹L A S S O         E
     C    N
     O
     P
     E
```

```
                    ¹D        ²B
                ³S O ⁴M B R E R O
                    A    O       O
               ⁵V E ⁶T E R A N   Z  ⁷S T Y
                    R    I    O      H
                    U   ⁸S C A L D
                    C        L    E
                   ⁹E L O P E
```

4. description

```
  ¹V E ²T E ³R I N ⁴A R I A N
   E    O   E      M
  ⁵S L I T ⁶V A M P I ⁷R E
   V       O        H  E
   E      ⁸L A R I A T
   T       V        B  U
           E       ⁹T I A R A
           R        A  N
                    N
```

5. mixed

References and
Recommended Bibliography

Bond, G.L., and Wagner, E.B. *Teaching the Child To Read.* New York: Macmillan, 1966.

Bruner, J.S. *The Process of Education.* New York: Random House, Vintage Books, 1960.

Carrillo, Lawrence W. *Teaching Reading: A Handbook.* New York: St. Martin's Press, 1976.

Chall, Jeanne S. *Learning To Read: The Great Debate.* New York: McGraw-Hill, 1967.

Clarke School for the Deaf. *Reading.* Northampton, Mass., 1972.

D'Arcy, Pat. *Reading for Meaning—Vol. 1: Learning To Read.* London: Hutchinson Ed. Ltd., 1973.

Dolch, E.W. *Psychology and Teaching of Reading.* Westport, Conn.: Greenwood, 1951.

Durkin, D. *Teaching Them To Read.* Boston: Allyn & Bacon, Inc., 1974.

Ekwall, E.E. *Diagnosis and Remediation of the Disabled Reader.* Boston: Allyn & Bacon, Inc., 1976.

Fries, C.C. *Linguistics and Reading.* New York: Holt, Rinehart and Winston, 1962.

Furth, H.G. *Thinking Without Language.* New York: Free Press, 1966.

Gates, A.I. *Manual of Directions for the Gates Reading Readiness Tests.* New York: Bureau of Publications, Teachers College, Columbia University, 1942.

Gibson, E., and Levin, H. *The Psychology of Reading.* Boston: M.I.T. Press, 1975.

Goodman, K.S., and Niles, O.S. *Reading: Process and Program.* Champaign, Ill.: National Council of Teachers of English, 1970.

Gray, W.S. *On Their Own in Reading.* Chicago: Scott, Foresman and Co., 1960.

Gunderson, Doris V., Ed. *Language and Reading.* Washington, D.C.: Center for Applied Linguistics, 1970.

Harris, A.J. *How To Increase Reading Ability.* McKay, 1975.

Heilman, A.W., and Holmes, E.A. *Smuggling Language into the Teaching of Reading.* Columbus, Ohio: Charles E. Merrill, 1972.

Hildreth, G. *Teaching Reading: A Guide to Basic Principles and Modern Practices.* New York: Holt, Rinehart & Winston, 1958.

Kavanagh, J.F., and Mattingly, I.G. (Eds.). *Language by Ear and by Eye.* Boston: M.I.T. Press, 1974.

Kavanagh, M.M., Ed. *Communicating by Language: The Reading Process.* Bethesda, Md.: NICH, 1968.

Kohl, H. *Reading, How To.* New York: E.P. Dutton, 1973.

Kottmeyer, W. *Teacher's Guide for Remedial Reading.* New York: McGraw-Hill, 1959.

Levin, H., and Williams, J. (Eds.). *Basic Studies on Reading.* New York: Basic, 1970.

Monroe, M. *Growing into Reading.* Westport, Conn.: Greenwood, 1951.

New York State Education Department. *Child Development Guide.* Albany, N.Y., 1955.

O'Brien, C.A. *Teaching the Language-Different Child to Read.* Columbus, Ohio: Charles E. Merrill, 1973.

Pintner, R., Eisenson, J., and Stanton, M. *The Psychology of the Physically Handicapped.* New York: F.S. Crofts & Co., 1945.

Reasoner, Charles F. *Releasing Children to Literature: A Teacher's Guide to Yearling Books.* New York: Dell, 1968.

Rosenstein, J. See *Bibliography on Deafness*, Washington, D.C.: A. G. Bell Association for the Deaf, 1977, for *Volta Review* contributions.

Russell, David, et al. *Reading Aids Through the Grades.* New York: Teachers College, Columbia University, 1975.

Schonell, F.J., and Goodacre, E. *The Psychology and Teaching of Reading.* New York: Longman, 1974.

Scott, Foresman Reading System, Level 4. "John and His Drum," illustrated by Ramon Orellana. Glenview, Ill., 1971.

Smith F. *Psycholinguistics and Reading.* New York: Holt, Rinehart & Winston, 1973.

Smith, N.B. (Ed.) *Reading Methods and Teacher Improvement.* Newark, Del.: International Reading Assn., 1971.

Spache, George D. *Diagnosing and Correcting Reading Disabilities.* Boston: Allyn & Bacon, 1976.

Strang, R. et al. *Improvement of Reading.* New York: McGraw-Hill, 1967.

Streng, A. *Reading for Deaf Children.* Washington, D.C.: The Alexander Graham Bell Assn. for the Deaf, 1964.

Tinker, M.A. *Teaching Elementary Reading.* New York: Prentice-Hall, 1975.